Camden
Town

HIGH STREET, CAMDEN TOWN.

Camden Town

Dreams of Another London

Tom Bolton

For Jo

'Another England there I saw,
Another London with its Tower'
'The Crystal Cabinet', William Blake, 1804

'Nothing between Morden and Camden Town holds terror for me.'
Angela Carter, 'Adventures at the End of Time',
London Review of Books, 7 March 1991

First published in 2017 by
The British Library
96 Euston Road
London NW1 2DB

British Library Cataloguing in Publication Data A catalogue record for
this book is available from the British Library

ISBN: 978 0 7123 5694 7

Titlepage: Postcard of Camden High Street, 1903

Typeset by IDSUK (DataConnection) Ltd
Cover by Sandra Friesen Design
Picture research by Sally Nicholls
Printed in Italy by Lego S.p.A.

Contents

View of Camden Market, 2015.

Introduction

Camden Town can seem like the only place in London to be. Summer sunset on Camden Lock, groups leaning on the rails watching the barges; the Victorian labyrinth of the Lock Market, squeezed into oddly shaped corners and hidden courtyards; the dome of the Roundhouse rising over the railway lines like a North London Pantheon; pubs in every direction, each for a different tribe; records, book and comic shops still, if you know where to look; the High Street lined with folk art signs in the form of giant boots and façade-crawling dragons; music in all directions, from bands in the back rooms of pubs last redecorated in the 1970s to venues of choice for whoever is in town – Koko and the Jazz Café, Cecil Sharp House and Green Note, the Fiddler's Elbow and the London Irish Centre, Dingwall's, the Underworld beneath the World's End pub, the Dublin Castle, Camden Assembly. All you need is within the compass of three stops on the Northern Line – celebrated Camden Town, famously obscure Mornington Crescent, and elegant, art nouveau Chalk Farm.

Camden Town can also seem like the last place in London to be. The seedy Lock with its jostling undercurrent of menace; French teenagers and Spanish punks ripped off by fake weed salesmen; market stalls with all the appeal and originality of Oxford Street tourist shops, selling souvenirs of when Camden was different; over-priced, over-hyped pubs running on the fumes of their reputations; an alternative cultural scene, once influential and important, now sold-up or selling out; packed streets and overcrowded venues; bad bands in worse cellars; shameful

Exterior view of the Roundhouse, 2016.

poverty, bad housing, people who have never seen the Thames; street sleepers and shop doorway drinkers; 3am assaults, gang fights, murders; gentrification and celebrity show ponies. And too many overcrowded tube stations.

Of course it is all of these things, usually at the same time. Camden Town can be the centre of everything, and the only neighbourhood that really embodies the unpredictable cultural mix on which London likes to pride itself. It can just as easily embody the worst of the socially divided, commodified, monetised, privatised clone city. Camden Town is where the soul of post-industrial, twenty-first century London can be found, for better and for worse.

This book takes five places, all unmistakable Camden landmarks, as starting points for a series of journeys into the layers of history and culture that are Camden Town. The World's End pub, once the Mother Red Cap, has existed in various forms since before Camden began, and is the place around which Camden still pivots. The Regent's Canal Bridge is Camden's tourist mecca, where crowds swirl around the canal locks and the market. Arlington House is only a block from the Lock Market, but belongs to a separate, parallel Camden of immigration and new beginnings, poverty and homelessness. No. 8 Royal College Street, bolt-hole for the poets Rimbaud and Verlaine, links the first buildings of the nineteenth-century Camden Town suburb to the social outsiders being attracted here from early on. Finally, the Roundhouse is an engineering curiosity that became the revered centre of Camden's cultural scene, sending out ripples way beyond the Chalk Farm Road. These are five ways to think about a place that is impossible, unmistakable and essential to London's future psychological balance.

A Gentleman
Vsher wᵗʰₐ
white Rodd

The Coate borne by
William Cambden
Clarenceux King
of Armes.

A Gentleman
Vsher wᵗʰ a
white rodd.

Detail from an early seventeenth-century manuscript describing Elizabeth I's funeral procession. In the centre is William Camden, wearing the official robes of the Clarenceux King of Arms.

Chapter 1 **From Camden's Origins to its Darkest Places**

London first emerges from the mists of the past in sketch form. The earliest representations of the city are the panoramic drawings that appeared in the Tudor era, pre-dating the first maps. Anthony van den Wyngaerde's *Panorama of London, Westminster and Southwark*, from 1543, shows us Henry VIII's city in scratchy, tantalising perspective drawing. The City of London is entirely contained within its walls, and beyond there are only isolated settlements – monasteries, farmsteads and moated manor houses scattered among distant trees. Van den Wyngaerde installed himself on the south bank, looking north over the Thames to the Hampstead Ridge on the horizon across a space that was yet to be occupied by North London. Between the City and the high ground, generic representations of trees and fields fill the space where Camden Town will eventually bloom.

The only location recognisable from pre-modern Camden is the junction site where the World's End pub, formerly the Mother Red Cap, is now found. The meeting point between the road to Hampstead and the road to Kentish Town was the only feature that distinguished this place on the long route out of London. The junction was a stopping place long before there was anything else. Camden Town grew from this meeting point, and centuries later it remains the undisputed centre. The story of how farming country beyond the city walls became the dark heart of modern London, seething with the horror of the city, is the story of how Camden Town came to be.

Before Camden

The early history of the place that was to become Camden Town is scanty. The first Garter King at Arms, Sir William Bruges, had a country estate in Kentish Town. As chief herald in Britain, his position gave him a senior diplomatic role in the Royal Household. He was part of Henry V's victorious army at the Battle of Agincourt and in 1416, a few months after the battle, he hosted King Sigismund, who visited Britain to negotiate an alliance against France. Sigismund, a European monarch extraordinaire, was King of Germany at the time. He had previously been King of Bohemia, and would later become King of Hungary and Croatia, and eventually Holy Roman Emperor. Sigismund's party probably travelled from the Bishop of Ely's Holborn residence, along the Hampstead and Kentish Town Roads (through future Camden Town) to Bruges's estate, where they feasted handsomely. Bruges Place, off Royal College Street, is a modern reminder of Camden's medieval power broker.

After this cameo appearance in international relations, the area relapsed into obscurity. By the late seventeenth century small settlements ringed the open spaces around the road to Hampstead, where streets were yet to be laid out. St Pancras lay to the south-east and Marylebone to the west, as hamlets gathered around their churches. Holloway, on the main road to the north, was recorded as a village from the 1300s. On the hills to the north, the village of Hampstead traced its origins back to Ethelred the Unready. And to the north-west, Kentish Town, beside the River Fleet, was known as a hamlet in the time of King John, well before William Bruges. Kentish Town was perhaps named after somebody called Kentish, or after a ditch containing the River Fleet, but explanations are lost in the far, Celtic past. The name does not seem to have anything to do with Kent, being on entirely the wrong side of London.

In the pre-railway age, the fields between London and Kentish Town were part of the arduous journey out of London towards Hertfordshire. As late as 1813, the Prince Regent was caught in a

'Camden Town, From the Hampstead Road, Marylebone, 1780', in George Walter Thornbury, *Old and New London*, Cassell & Co., 1887–93..

thick fog on his way to Hatfield House, turning back when one of his party fell into a ditch 'at the entrance of Kentish Town, which at that time was not lit with gas, and probably not even with oil'.[1]

The most significant feature of the landscape was Primrose Hill, a wooded hilltop (until its trees were chopped down during the seventeenth century). Lord Southampton, who owned the land on the west side of Camden High Street, laid out building plots, and streets of Italianate houses began to appear over the course of the nineteenth century. The top of the hill, though, became public space and remained open ground, cross-hatched with paths, but retaining just a hint of its former wildness.

The oldest London settlements, such as Hackney, Hampstead and Islington, were built on well-drained sand and gravel where the soil was good and springs plentiful. The River Fleet flowed through where Camden would be, on its way from the Hampstead Ridge down to Holborn and the Thames. It carved a valley from Kentish Town to St Pancras, along the eastern edge of Camden. The land here still drops sharply from Royal College Street down to the thalweg (the lowest point of a river valley). The land at Camden was heavy, packed with the stiff riverbank London clay that drags and clings. The London clay fields were the last spaces on the map to be filled in, with Victorian suburbs such as Notting Hill, St John's Wood and Camden Town only being built after better options had been exhausted.

For centuries Camden was a space between Holborn and the Hampstead Ridge, with no pressing qualities to attract residents, and it was a long time before its value became apparent.

A Name and Two Junctions

Tudor antiquarian William Camden suggested that 'Antiquity has told us nothing of the first Founder of this City; as indeed Cities, growing up by little and little, do seldom know their original'.[2] In fact Camden Town is named, indirectly, after William Camden himself. Everything in Camden flows through the junction at the World's End, where five roads radiate around the compass. Camden's flesh hangs from these bones. Although no one uses its official title, it is known to Camden Council as 'Britannia Junction'. It is named after William Camden's *Britannia*, the first descriptive survey of the nation. Beginning in 1587, Camden recorded detailed descriptions of the landscape and history of Britain and Ireland in his spare time, while working his way up to become Headmaster of Westminster School. His publications brought him fame and a heraldic appointment as Clarenceux King of Arms, and he is depicted looking smooth in his robes of office as part of the funeral procession for Elizabeth I.

Although William Camden's life and work preceded Camden Town by a couple of hundred years, he is connected in a circuitous manner. He retired to a manor in Chislehurst which, after his death, was named Camden Place. During the late eighteenth century, Sir Charles Pratt lived at Camden Place. Pratt became Lord Chancellor and a protector of civil liberties, serving under Prime Ministers William Pitt the Elder and the Duke of Grafton, and was raised to the peerage as Baron Camden and then Earl of Camden, taking his titles from his Chislehurst seat. Camden Town was built on Pratt's land, and so Britannia Junction neatly connects the place back to its origins.

Charles Pratt was also indirectly responsible for Camden Town's sister city in New Jersey, on the opposite bank of the Delaware to Philadelphia. Founded in 1773, the town was named after the Earl of Camden who, as Lord Chancellor, was appreciated for defending the colonies from taxation without representation. The twenty-first-century version, Camden, N.J., suffers from post-industrial decay and high crime rates, and has become notorious as supposedly 'the worst town in America'.

London's Camden Town is strewn with Lord Camden's spare family names, including his second title, Viscount Bayham, and his wife's surname, Jeffreys, plus her home town of Brecknock, which gave his son the title of the Earl of Brecknock. Bayham and

Pratt Streets hold the Camden grid together. Brecknock Primary School marks the outer reaches of Camden Road, while north of the Regent's Canal are Jeffreys Street and Jeffreys Place.

Charles Pratt acquired his Camden estates through marriage – his wife was a descendant of Judge Jeffreys, of Bloody Assizes fame. Camden therefore owes its origins to one of London's favourite folk villains. Just as Pratt was later to do, Jeffreys served as Lord Chancellor and was created Baron Jeffreys by James II. He is forever associated with the 1689 Bloody Assizes, the trials at which he sent around 170 people to the gallows following the Monmouth Rebellion against King James.

By the eighteenth century, the fields of Camden were estate property. The west side of what is now Camden High Street belonged to the Earl of Southampton, who also owned the land to the south between Camden and Bloomsbury, on which Somers Town was later built. The east side belonged to the Earls of Camden (Charles Pratt and his descendants). Several other estates divided up neighbouring territory – Belsize Manor, Hampstead Manor, Kilburn Priory, the Cantelowes Estate on the road to Kentish Town, and the Chalcots Estate which encompassed Primrose Hill and later gave rise to the name Chalk Farm.

A single route, Hampstead Road, crossed Camden north to south. Cary's map of 1795 shows Camden Town just before it germinated.[3] Britannia Junction exists in nascent form, a fork with Kentish Town Road. An evidently muddy path, Slipshoe Lane, marks the line of modern Parkway. Further south there is a second junction where Fig Lane, later Crowndale Road, arrives from St Pancras. This is the Cobden Junction in its earliest form, where Mornington Crescent tube station is now located. The high street between these two junctions remains the spine of Camden Town.

Remarkably, Camden includes a direct business link to this era. Founded in St Pancras in 1789, funeral directors Leverton & Sons moved to its current offices on Eversholt Street in 1888. The firm is Funeral Director to the Royal Household, and organised the state funerals of Princess Diana and the Queen Mother.

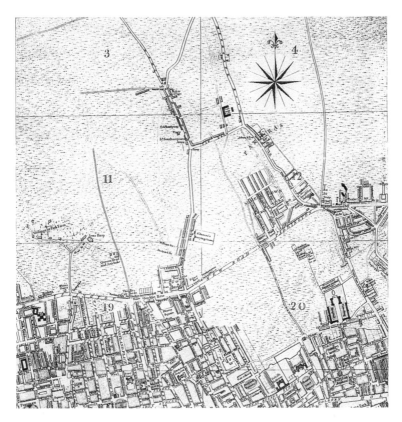

Detail showing the area we now know as Camden from *Cary's New and Accurate Plan of London and Westminster*, 1795. Published by John Cary, London. The last building before the roads fork at the top, clearly labelled, is the Mother Red Cap pub. Today the forked roads are Camden High Street (left) and Kentish Town Road (right), meeting at the tube station.

Camden's Skeleton

In 1791 the Earl of Camden began the development of Camden Town, leasing land east of the High Street for the construction of houses. However, it was some years before development got underway, and the 1795 map mentioned above shows only a handful of buildings hugging the Hampstead Road between the two junctions. Only three individual buildings are named – a Veterinary College, away to the east on a street later to become Royal College Street; Mother Red Cap pub at the south-east corner of Britannia Junction; and Lord Southampton's Arms at Cobden Junction. Other maps of the period label the junction as 'The Mother Black Caps', after a pub that was opposite the Mother Red Cap, on the site now occupied by Camden Town tube station.

By 1804, Thompson's map of St Pancras shows the fields starting to fill, and Camden emerging. Buildings can be seen along Camden High Street, from Fig Lane to the Mother Red Cap. In its first incarnation, Camden High Street (which changed its name from Hampstead Road in 1863) was a row of two-storey buildings 'separated by hedges of privet' from the street.[4] In 1822, the name Camden Town appeared on a map for the first time, and Camden could be finally be said to exist as a place in its own right.

Camden took definitive shape in the 1830s, when its core grid was laid out, comprising ten streets that still form the bulk of modern Camden Town. Six run north–south – Arlington Street, Camden High Street, Bayham Street, Camden Street, Royal College Street and St Pancras Way. Four run east–west – Crowndale Road, Plender Street, Pratt Street and Camden Road/ Parkway. Some had different names when first built, but the layout is essentially unaltered.

The centrepiece of the new town was intended to be Camden Square, away towards Kentish Town Road with a new street, Camden Road, built especially to provide access. It developed slowly. In 1849 there was a church, St Paul's, and little else. In 1860 the east side of the square still had no houses, but by 1871 it was finally finished. Its completion was driven by Charles Pratt's son, John, a politician like his father. He had served as Lord Lieutenant of Ireland and in return received a title upgrade, going from Earl to Marquess of Camden.

The villas and terraces of the square are the grandest houses in Camden Town – four storeys, cream and pink, and still the best address Camden has to offer. When Amy Winehouse moved to No. 30 Camden Square in 2011, she had reached the top of the Camden ladder, but she would only spend four months there before her untimely death. St Paul's Church, however, has gone. It was bombed in the war and replaced with a temporary, utilitarian shed which is still there seventy years on, a reminder of the imperfect London beyond the confines of Camden Square.

No. 62 Camden Square was the location of Britain's first weather station. G. J. Symons, editor of *Symons's Meteorological Magazine*, set up a pioneering monitoring station in his garden to measure rainfall, and his house became the headquarters of the British Rainfall Organisation. In 1922 the Royal Meteorological Society acquired the organisation and the property, and continued to use the equipment. The house was rented out, from 1938 to 1952, to the West Africa Students Union, but residents were still obliged to take regular rainfall measurements. The station moved to the central gardens in Camden Square in 1957, and provided reports until 1969.

The west side of Camden was developed by Charles Fitzroy, Earl of Southampton. The plots leased on his land were smaller, leading to the narrower, more modest terraces of Mornington Terrace, Albert Street and Arlington Road. This model spread beyond the New Town, and terraces became the defining Camden building type. According to historian Stephen Inwood, 'The whole area between Albany Street . . . and Pancras Road was filled with mediocre housing for clerks, artisans and workmen'.[5]

The junction at Mornington Crescent tube station marks the south end of Camden High Street, just as Britannia Junction and Camden Town tube station mark the north end. It is known as Cobden

Junction, after the statue of anti-Corn Laws MP Richard Cobden. Providing a slightly strange neighbourhood focal point, the statue was mostly financed by Napoleon III – who, after losing the Franco-Prussian War in 1870, was living in exile at none other than Camden Place, William Camden's former Chislehurst home.

The choice of location for the statue seems to be a mystery. Richard Cobden came from Sussex and was a Manchester MP, but his name is nevertheless attached to a pub and a primary school as well as the junction. However, twenty years after the statue was put up, Cobden's daughter Eleanor married Walter Sickert, who lived a mere flick of a paintbrush from the statue in Mornington Crescent. It is now badly weathered, giving the godfather of free trade an alarmingly cadaverous appearance.

Camden Town in Ten Pubs

The new suburb began life as a street with pubs at either end, and the pubs of Camden Town are perhaps the best indication of its elusive essence of place. By 1830, Camden was home to ten pubs. As well as the Mother Red Cap, the Mother Black Cap and the Southampton Arms, there were the Bedford Arms, the Britannia, the Camden Arms, the Elephant & Castle, the Hope & Anchor, the Laurel Tree and the Wheatsheaf.

Five of these pubs have survived and five have closed. The fate of these original pubs provides a pocket guide to twenty-first-century Camden Town, much of which would still be recognisable to an early Victorian. Built around a nineteenth-century core, the history and fate of Camden's original drinking places are representative of the place it is today.

The five lost pubs are the Britannia, the Hope & Anchor, the Elephant & Castle, the Mother Black Cap and the Bedford. The Britannia occupied the corner building at Britannia Junction on Camden High Street and Parkway. The ground floor has been rebuilt as shops, but a figure of Britannia still keeps watch, seated between the fourth-floor windows. The Hope & Anchor on Crowndale Road closed controversially in 2013 and was then squatted. It awaits conversion to housing.

Demolished after the Second World War, the Elephant & Castle was located opposite St Pancras Workhouse (now St Pancras Hospital). Local nineteenth-century historian, Samuel Palmer, claimed that it took its name from the Palaeolithic remains of what he described as an elephant found near the workhouse in the buried River Fleet in 1714. John Conyers, an apothecary and antiquarian digger, supervised the excavations (which also uncovered the 'Gray's Inn Lane handaxe', now in the British Museum). The elephant was probably a mammoth, but Conyers surmised that the Romans had brought elephants to Britain with them to scare the locals.

The Elephant's Head pub, which now operates on the High Street, has no pre-historic connections and is named after the logo of the defunct Camden Brewery. The brewery closed in 1926, having been absorbed by Courage after a coin toss with Barclay Perkins to decide who took the spoils. The former headquarters building on the corner of Hawley Crescent and Kentish Town Road has an elephant over its front door in brick relief. Camden's elephants can be traced all the way back to the Pratt family's coat of arms, which includes three white elephant heads on a black field, said to symbolise power, fidelity and wisdom. A single elephant now sits on the London Borough of Camden's crest wearing a holly wreath around its neck, imported from arms of the defunct Borough of Hampstead.

The Mother Black Cap closed in 2015, amid angry protests. It became a gay pub during the 1960s and developed into a legendary burlesque venue, the 'Palladium of Drag'. It was temporarily reopened by squatters, and campaigners have so far fought off attempts to reopen it as a chain restaurant. Ironically, given its actual history, a fictionalised Mother Black Cap features in the film *Withnail and I* as a terrifyingly unreconstructed boozer. The film's title characters order 'Two large gins. Two pints of cider. Ice in the cider' – a ludicrous proposition, at least when the film was released – and are alarmed by sexually threatening graffiti in the Gents before being chased out by a huge Irishman, with whom they foolishly make eye contact. The scene was, however, filmed in a now-demolished pub in Notting Hill.

The Bedford

The Bedford Arms was demolished in the late 1960s; its site at No. 88 Arlington Street is marked with an inscription. Known as the Bedford Tavern in the nineteenth century, it boasted a tea garden, a bowling green and a shrimp stall among other attractions – but was most famous for the daring balloon ascents made from its gardens. In 1824 a Mr Rossiter took off from the tavern garden, with an unnamed companion, and ascended through the clouds, reaching a height of 'about two miles and a quarter from the earth',[6] where they startled a pigeon and started to feel the chill. They ditched their ballast and land safely in Havering Park in Essex, where an unimpressed estate steward ordered them to leave. They then took a coach back, arriving at the Bedford before closing time. A little later, a Mr Graham caused even more excitement by ascending with two ladies, Mrs Graham and a Mrs Forbes, who were equipped with flags which they waved. They landed in Feltham, but disappointed the Bedford's clientele by taking a cab straight home rather than returning for a hero's welcome.

A music hall, the Bedford, was built in the pub's gardens and opened in 1861. Facing onto Camden High Street, for a century it was the most prominent building on the street and a Camden Town landmark. It burned down in 1899, but was rebuilt on the same site with a dome, a canopied entrance and signs declaring it 'The Bedford Palace of Varieties'.

Both the old theatre and its replacement were the subject of numerous works by Camden-based painter Walter Sickert, who lived at No. 6 Mornington Crescent (where a blue plaque marks his former home) and rented various properties in Camden Town. Strongly influenced by the Impressionists, he visited the Bedford frequently during the 1890s to paint its gas lit interior. His pictures draw on Edgar Degas's paintings of dancers and audiences in Paris, but with an added layer of Camden grime. Sickert painted the crowds in the gilt galleries and boxes, and the performers on the stage. He captured the heavy clothing, the heavy atmosphere and the warm, alluring glow of the stage.

Sickert's music-hall performers are the first stars of Camden Town. His most famous work depicts the red-coated and red-hatted Minnie Cunningham, who dressed as a schoolgirl and, according to Marie Lloyd, sang 'romping schoolgirl songs' in a style that we would find rather disturbing.[7] One of her songs, for example, contained the line 'I'm an old hand at love, though I'm young in years'. For years the painting was described as 'Minnie Cunningham at the Old Bedford', but it has recently been suggested that it is actually of a performance at the Tivoli on the Strand, robbing Camden of its most iconic image. However, plenty of other Sickert works undoubtedly show the Bedford, including pictures of child singer Little Dot Hetherington and Yorkshire cockney singer Vesta Victoria. Sickert carried on painting the rebuilt theatre until the First World War.

At the height of music hall's popularity, its most popular performers frequented the Bedford stage, including 'Champagne Charlie' George Leybourne, male impersonator Vesta Tilley, and Crazy Gang comedian Jimmy Nervo. Others made early appearances at the Bedford, with both Charlie Chaplin and Gracie Fields performing there in 1912. As a small boy Peter Sellers lived over the theatre in 1929 while his parents were performing below in a review called *Ha! Ha! Ha!*, after which his father did a runner.

The 'Queen of the Music Hall' was Marie Lloyd, and the Bedford was her favourite place to play. Lloyd's near forty-year career spanned music hall at its peak, and her cheerful, bucktoothed performances of innuendo-heavy comic songs define the genre. Her earliest success was in 1885 with 'The Boy I Love is Up in the Gallery', for which she stationed her little sister in the gods with a handkerchief to wave at the key moment. One of her final successes was in 1919, with 'My Old Man Said Follow the Van'. Lloyd collapsed on stage at the Alhambra, Leicester Square, in 1922 and died shortly after at the age of fifty-two. In 1898 Charles Booth's social survey reported that No. 80 King's Road (later St Pancras Road) had been 'recently vacated by Marie Lloyd'.[8] She may have moved on for classier surroundings, as the survey also reports brothels at Nos 131 and 133.

After a short time as a cinema in the 1930s, the Bedford became a playhouse. It closed in 1951, despite attempts to revive its flagging fortunes with repertory theatre. Some of its final productions that year were under the management of Sir Donald Wolfit, who gave both his King Lear and his Othello. Both theatre and actor-manager had become relics of a lost era.

The 1949 British musical comedy film *Trottie True*, filmed in the Bedford, harks back to the glory days. It tells the story of an 1890s Gaiety Girl who has an affair with a balloonist, before eventually becoming a duchess. The Bedford makes a highly poignant final appearance in the 1967 film *The London Nobody Knows*, with presenter James Mason picking his way through its derelict interior. It was pulled down shortly after, and the site – Nos 93-95 Camden High Street – is now occupied by the Camden Job Centre.

The Pubs that Survived

The remaining five 1830s pubs are still serving today, although all their names have been changed. The Laurel Tree, on Greenland Street, is now Brewdog. The Wheatsheaf, on the High Street, is currently Belushi's. The Southampton Arms became the Lyttelton Arms, renamed in tribute to jazz trumpeter and *I'm Sorry I Haven't a Clue* radio host Humphrey Lyttelton. Willie Rushton, regular panellist on the show, is memorialised with a plaque over the

View of the stage and auditorium in the derelict Bedford Theatre, shortly before its demolition in 1969.

road in Mornington Crescent tube station. The Radio Four show conferred cult status on Mornington Crescent with its game of the same name, in which contestants take turns to 'play' London locations. There are no rules except that the winner is the first to mention 'Mornington Crescent', and that the game has to be taken very seriously.

The Camden Arms, on Randolph Street, became the Colonel Fawcett. It was re-named after the victim of possibly the third last fatal duel fought in Britain. In 1843 Lieutenant-Colonel David Fawcett, newly returned from China, argued with his brother-in-law, Colonel Alexander Munro, over property. They fought a duel in a field by Camden Road, where Munro shot Fawcett in the chest. He was carried to the nearby Camden Arms, where he died. Munro, convicted of murder, fled the country, but eventually returned when his death sentence was commuted.

Controversially renamed the World's End in the 1980s, the Mother Red Cap is still to be found opposite Camden tube station on the site it has always occupied. Before there was Camden there was the Mother Red Cap, a tavern at the junction of the Hampstead and Kentish Town Roads. The eighteenth-century version of the inn had a tumbledown appearance and a sign swinging from a gibbet-like frame, showing an aged, forbidding woman in a Puritan hat. It was a stopping point in empty countryside, halfway between Hampstead and London, and it was reported in the 1840s that 'The "Mother Red-cap" at Kentish Town, was a house of no small terror to travellers in former times'.[9] It certainly possessed an impressive stock of alarming tales.

The inn seems to have developed a reputation as a default location for shady doings. It was, legend asserts, the home of 'Mother Damnable'. While 'Mother Red Cap' was an antiquated term for an old woman, or specifically a pub landlady, 'Mother Damnable' referred to an old woman with a reputation as either a witch or a procuress, or both. The nickname remained in use long enough to be applied to a notorious madame in 1890s Seattle. Camden's 'Mother Damnable' was supposedly Jinney

'The Old "Mother Red Cap" in 1746', in Edward Walford, *Old and New London: Volume 5*, Cassell, Petter & Galpin, 1878.

Mother Damnable of Kentish Town, Anno 1676. From a Unique Print in the Collection of J. Bindley Esqr. Published by I. Caulfield, 1793.

Bingham, the seventeenth-century criminal moll and consort of 'Gypsy' George Coulter, who 'lived no-one knew how'.[10] Jinney ran the inn as an underworld hang-out, and ran through a succession of men. When Gipsy George was hanged for sheep stealing, he was succeeded by a drinker called Darby. After Jinney and her mother 'consulted together', he vanished.[11] And a man called Pitcher, Jinney's final partner, was found burned to death in her oven. She was supposedly acquitted of his murder, claiming he had hidden there to escape her shrewish tongue.

Jinney's Kentish Town brickmaker father was said to have built the isolated inn. Both he and her mother, a Scottish pedlar's daughter, were supposedly hanged for causing the death of a young woman through witchcraft. On her death, 'hundreds of men, women and children were witnesses of the devil entering her house', according to Camden antiquary Samuel Palmer.[12] The devil did not come out again, and Jinney was found inside slumped over a teapot containing a lethal herbal brew.

These stories are entertainingly detailed, but at the very least involve the conflation of different people and the embellishment of facts. Palmer, who brought the Mother Red Cap tales together into a single story, claimed vaguely that it was 'given in an old pamphlet', which could be read as local history code for 'invented'.[13] However, variations on the story have been faithfully repeated ever since. It is seems more than appropriate that the pub is now called the World's End, with the Underworld venue lurking in the basement beneath.

Camden's Doom

Camden Town's folk reputation as a place of ill-repute, which dates from when it was just a lonely traveller's rest, persisted into the industrial era and beyond. Mother Shipton, supposed author of sixteenth-century prophecies, is often quoted as claiming that 'When London surrounds Primrose Hill, the streets of the

Metropolis will run with blood', associating the emergence of Camden Town with the end of times. However, William Blake countered these gloomy omens with his vision of Jerusalem in NW1:

The fields from Islington to Marybone
To Primrose Hill and Saint John's Wood
Were builded over with pillars of gold
And there Jerusalem's pillars stood.

He gets more specific, describing how:

Pancras and Kentish Town repose
Among her golden pillars high
Among her golden arches which
Shine upon the starry sky.[14]

Although he does not know it, Blake's vision is of Camden Town. However, it is Mother Shipton whom Camden chose to commemorate, naming a pub on Prince of Wales Road after her (now the Fiddler's Elbow).

Before the railways, London, just as much of the rest of Britain, was a smaller, more confined place. Camden was the nearest open space north of town, and for an ordinary Londoner 'to pass a day in the fields of Camden and Kentish Town, or perhaps venture as far as the hill of Highgate, was the boundary of his wishes' according to Samuel Palmer. Palmer points out, however, that 'the only drawback to the enjoyment of this pleasure was the total absence of an organised police',[15] ensuring that as night fell the countryside became a place of unmistakable danger.

Primrose Hill was the site of a notorious murder in 1678. One evening in October, magistrate Sir Edmund Berry Godfrey failed to return home to his house near the Strand. His body was discovered by the landlord of the White House pub (later the Chalk Farm Tavern), face down in a ditch on the south side of the hill, a sword in his back. Godfrey was embroiled in the Titus Oates conspiracy, an attempt to stoke anti-Catholic sentiment through false accusations of a French plot against Charles II. Oates made an ever-increasing string of accusations, naming more than eighty high profile Catholics as part of an assassination conspiracy. Godfrey had taken his affidavit, and his murder added credibility to the accusations and fed the paranoia sweeping the nation. A dagger commemorating Godfrey's murder, inscribed 'Remember religion', became a best seller. Titus Oates was given a squad of soldiers, and with his Whig supporters began rounding up the accused, fifteen of whom were executed. It was three years before Parliament accepted that Titus Oates had made it all up. In 1679 three men, called Green, Berry and Hill, were executed on Primrose Hill, denounced by a servant to the Queen, Miles Prance, who claimed they had stabbed Godfrey at Somerset House as part of a Catholic conspiracy, and dumped his body at Primrose Hill. However, Prance later retracted his account and the murder remains unsolved, the subject of several books which have advanced political theories for the killing.

The court records of the eighteenth century include several cases of violent robbery and assault on the roads between Holborn and Kentish Town. In 1773, for example, the *London Courant* reported that 'On Thursday night some villains robbed the Kentish Town stage, and stripped the passengers of their money, watches, and buckles.'[16] The journey through empty country evidently made travellers nervous. In 1786 two women were robbed by one John Price. All he had to do was approach them with his hat pulled over his eyes, crying 'Make haste, make haste,' at which they handed over 'half a guinea, a new shilling and a sixpence'.[17] His accomplice was, it was revealed in court, carrying a concealed pistol, but it was not required. Price was convicted of robbery and hanged, and he was not the only one. Old St Pancras Churchyard contains an inscription to 'John Fowler. Highwayman, shot near Camden Town' in 1703, in a failed robbery near the Mother Red Cap.

Camden is also associated, a little vaguely, with Moll Cutpurse. An historical figure, Moll was an Elizabethan celebrity whose real name was Mary Frith. She developed a reputation not only for dressing in men's clothes, complete with sword, but for behaving like a man too – robbing, fencing, pimping, drinking, smoking and singing songs to theatre audiences, accompanying herself on the lute. Her legend was in full swing during her lifetime, with two contemporary plays written about her. Thomas Dekker and Thomas Middleton's *The Roaring Girl* has proved popular in the modern repertoire, but the other, by John Day, entitled *The Madde Pranckes of Mery Mall of the Bankside*, is sadly lost. We will never know whether it delivered on the promise of its title, nor can we tell from where the nineteenth-century writers who claimed Moll performed regularly at the Mother Red Cap obtained their information. However, the pub certainly attracts tales about dangerous women that are too good to ignore.

The Camden Town Murder

The dark legends of Camden are supplemented by a darker reality. During the early twentieth century, the heyday of poisonings and stranglings, murder fiction and lurid press coverage, Camden became associated with a series of gruesome killings for which, it was implied, the place itself was partly to blame. The Camden Town Murder of 1907 was a prime example. Phyllis Dimmock was found lying in bed at 29 St Paul's Road (now Agar Grove) with her throat cut from ear to ear, and the remains of a shared supper on the table. Phyllis was really Emily from Hertfordshire, who had come to London to work in service but ended up working as a prostitute in the netherworld of King's Cross, which was a red-light district then as it would be a century later. A brothel keeper, John Crabtree, in whose house off Euston Road she had rented a room, gave the police a description that fitted a young man called Robert Wood. He was a commercial glass designer with 'artistic hands' who had been meeting Emily in secret. The week before he had given her a postcard in the Eagle pub on Royal College Street, signed with an alias. It said: 'Phillis darling. If it pleases you to meet me at 8.15 at the [here he drew a rising sun]. Yours to a cinder. Alice.' Emily was last seen in the Eagle with Wood, missing an assignation with a ship's cook called Robert Roberts with whom she had spent the previous three nights.

At this time Emily was twenty-two and lived with a man called Bert Shaw, aged twenty-one. They had set up house as Mr and Mrs Shaw on St Paul's Road. Bert had taken a job as a chef for the Midland Railway on the Sheffield Express, leaving Euston mid-afternoon and returning the next morning. Emily had given up prostitution, but not for long. Her new life did not suit her, and she was said to miss the entertainment of the Euston Road pubs. Bert was away on the Express the night she was killed. Robert Wood's assignation with Emily looked suspicious and, although the evidence against him was slim, he was arrested.

The case seemed straightforward, but it drew public attention as Wood's trial played out in the newly reopened Old Bailey. Wood's solicitor was Arthur Newton, who would later represent Dr Crippen. His defence counsel, Edward Marshall Hall, was a legendary performer, and the courts were a public exhibition that drew eager crowds who, if they were no longer allowed to attend executions, could at least enjoy the rest of the drama. Wood became the first defendant in a murder trial to give evidence on his own behalf. When asked if he had murdered Emily, he declared haughtily, 'Of course not. I mean it's ridiculous'. Witnesses were able to give him an alibi, Marshall Hall put in a searing cross-examination for the defence, and the judge ordered Wood's acquittal, by which time the crime was sensational public property.

Emily Dimmock's murder, which has never been solved, has become a classic mystery of its time. Strange circumstances swirl around the case, including the search for a soldier called Jumbo Large, whose name was supposedly revealed by Emily's spirit to her sister Rosa on the night of her death. The case has also become entangled with Britain's most infamous unsolved murders, the Jack the Ripper killings. Part of the blame lies with crime author Patricia Cornwell, who wrote a notoriously speculative book which laid the Ripper murders and the Camden Town Murder at the door of Walter Sickert. However, a little of the responsibility lies with Sickert himself, who first invited the connection in a powerful series of Camden paintings.

In 1908, the year after the Camden Town Murder, Sickert produced a series of paintings and drawings which became known as the Camden Town Murder series. With titles such as *The Camden Murder or What Shall We Do for the Rent?*, they show a man, or in one case a woman, standing over or sitting beside a naked woman on a bed. 'What Shall We Do for the Rent?' was a music hall refrain, but also implies a resort to prostitution. The pictures are intentionally ambiguous, with no visual indication that any murder has taken place. They are, however, definitely images of poverty. Sickert worked in 'third floor backs' in Camden – single rooms with only one window. They were small, depressing lodgings for those with little money to spare, but Sickert appreciated the light and shadow created by the single source of daylight.

Sickert later declared that 'It is said that we are a great literary nation but we really don't care about literature, we like films and we like a good murder. . . after all murder is as good a subject as any other'.[18] He was fascinated by unsolved crimes and loved speculating about who might have done them. The Camden Town Murder series are 'problem pictures', a short-lived Edwardian genre that presented ambiguous scenes in which social and cultural roles were held up to scrutiny. The narrative implied in the titles he gave to his work creates tension and social context, but it was also good publicity. The paintings side-step literal meaning, but that has not discouraged the Ripper industry, keen to entertain the least likely scenarios.

The Shifty Eyes of Dr Crippen

The story returns inevitably to the Bedford Theatre, the spiritual centre of turn-of-the-century Camden. In 1910, while local singer

Walter Richard Sickert, *The Camden Town Murder or What Shall We Do for the Rent?* Oil on canvas, *c.* 1908. Yale Centre for British Art.

Belle Elmore performed on stage, her husband Dr Hawley Harvey Crippen was spending his time with another woman, Ethel Neave, who came from Diss in Norfolk. Elmore's real name was Cora Turner (and before that, Kunigunde Mackamotzki), and she and Crippen came from Michigan. They had moved to London in 1897, where Cora pursued her stage career and Crippen worked for a homeopathic company. Their home was No. 39 Hilldrop Crescent, at the Holloway end of Camden Road (later destroyed by wartime bombing).

Sacked by the homeopaths, Dr Crippen took a job managing Drouet's Institution for the Deaf, a fraudulent practice located on Regent's Park Road, where he conned money from deaf people in exchange for 'a cure'. According to an investigator who posed as a patient, Crippen wore 'a shirt of startling hue' and 'a "diamond" as big as a marble'. However, he had 'flabby gills' and 'shifty eyes', and his face was 'a warning to all observant beholders'.[19]

It was while he was working at Drouet's that Crippen met Ethel, a typist, who had changed her name to Ethel Le Neve for added exoticism. Cora had apparently been having affairs with lodgers at Hilldrop Crescent, and Crippen took revenge with Ethel. In January 1910, Cora stopped being seen around. Crippen told anyone who asked that she had returned to the States, where she had died and been cremated. Ethel started wearing her jewellery.

When Scotland Yard questioned Crippen he admitted he had made this story up, claiming he was embarrassed because Cora had actually run away with an actor. Chief Inspector Walter Dew was satisfied with this explanation, but Crippen and Le Neve were unaware of this and fled in panic to Brussels and then Antwerp, where they boarded the SS *Montrose* for Canada. Their disappearance prompted four searches of No. 39 Hilldrop Crescent, where a torso was finally found under the basement, traces of the sedative scopolamine in the remains. The rest of the body was never found, but it was later established that Crippen had made a number of trips to the Regent's Canal carrying heavy bags, and had received a delivery of lime. This grew over time into

METROPOLITAN POLICE

MURDER

AND MUTILATION.

Portraits, Description and Specimen of Handwriting of HAWLEY HARVEY CRIPPEN, alias Peter Crippen, alias Franckel; and ETHEL CLARA LE NEVE, alias Mrs. Crippen, and Neave.

Wanted for the Murder of CORA CRIPPEN, otherwise Belle Elmore; Kunigunde Mackamotzki: Marsangar and Turner, on, or about, 2nd February last.

Description of Crippen. Age 50, height 5 ft. 3 or 4, complexion fresh, hair light brown, inclined sandy, scanty, bald on top, rather long scanty moustache, somewhat straggly, eyes grey, bridge of nose rather flat, false teeth, medium build, throws his feet outwards when walking. May be clean shaven or wearing a beard and gold rimmed spectacles, and may possibly assume a wig.

Sometimes wears a jacket suit, and at other times frock coat and silk hat. May be dressed in a brown jacket suit, brown hat and stand up collar (size 15).

Somewhat slovenly appearance, wears his hat rather at back of head.

Very plausible and quiet spoken, remarkably cool and collected demeanour.

Speaks French and probably German. Carries Firearms.

An American citizen, and by profession a Doctor.

Has lived in New York, Philadelphia, St. Louis, Detroit, Michigan, Coldwater, and other parts of America.

May obtain a position as assistant to a doctor or eye specialist, or may practise as an eye specialist, Dentist, or open a business for the treatment of deafness, advertising freely.

Has represented Munyon's Remedies, in various cities in America.

Description of Le Neve alias Neave.—A shorthand writer and typist, age 27, height 5 ft, 5, complexion pale, hair light brown (may dye same), large grey or blue eyes, good teeth, nice looking, rather long straight nose (good shape), medium build, pleasant, lady-like appearance. Quiet, subdued manner, talks quietly, looks intently when in conversation. A native of London.

Dresses well, but quietly, and may wear a blue serge costume (coat reaching to hips) trimmed heavy braid, about ⅜ inch wide, round edge, over shoulders and pockets. Three large braid buttons down front, about size of a florin. three small ones on each pocket, two on each cuff, several rows of stitching round bottom of skirt; or a light grey shadow-stripe costume, same style as above, but trimmed grey moire silk instead of braid, and two rows of silk round bottom of skirt; or a white princess robe with gold sequins; or a mole coloured striped costume with black moire silk collar; or a dark vieuxrose cloth costume, trimmed black velvet collar; or a light heliotrope dress.

May have in her possession and endeavour to dispose of same:—a round gold brooch, with points radiating zig-zag from centre, each point about an inch long, diamond in centre, each point set brilliants, the brooch in all being slightly larger than a half-crown: and two single stone diamond rings, and a diamond and sapphire (or ruby) ring, stones rather large.

Absconded 9th inst, and may have left, or will endeavour to leave the country.

Please cause every enquiry at Shipping Offices, Hotels, and other likely places and cause ships to be watched.

Information to be given to the Metropolitan Police Office, New Scotland Yard, London, S.W., or at any Police Station.

E. R. HENRY,
The Commissioner of Police of the Metropolis.

Metropolitan Police Office,
New Scotland Yard. 16th July 1910.

London Metropolitan Police handbill, issued 16 July 1910, describing murder suspects Dr Crippen and Ethel Le Neve.

the legend that Crippen threw Cora's head into the Thames in one of her own sequinned handbags.

Chief Inspector Dew sent a famous, pioneering telegraph message to the SS *Montrose*, to which the ship's captain replied: 'Have strong suspicions that Crippen London cellar murderer and accomplice are among saloon passengers. Moustache taken off, growing beard. Accomplice dressed as boy. Manner and build undoubtedly a girl.'[21] Dew overtook the *Montrose* on a faster ship, boarded in disguise in the St Lawrence River, and arrested Crippen and Le Neve. Dew reflected that 'Old Crippen took it quite well. He was always a bit of a philosopher. . . quite a likeable chap in his own way'.[22]

Crippen was hanged in 1910, thanks partly to the forensic analysis of Cora's remains by pathologist Bernard Spilsbury, who dramatically presented a portion of her torso bearing an identifying appendix scar to the jury in a pudding bowl. Le Neve, who was only charged as an accessory, was acquitted and lived the rest of her life mostly in Sydenham, where she died in 1967, 'a rather cantankerous old lady . . . most of the time with her dentures out'.[23] It was not until the 1980s, when a journalist came calling, that her children discovered who she really was.

Camden's Most Wanted

At the other end of the twentieth century and the opposite end of Camden, the Kentish Town Job Centre on Camden Road was where Dennis Nilsen worked as an Executive Officer in the early 1980s. After work he went out looking for men. He picked them up and took them back to his flat in Muswell Hill, where he often murdered them. In 1983 he was found guilty of six murders, although he had confessed to fifteen. He was said to be a keen cook, who on special occasions would make curries for his colleagues in the same large cooking pots he used for dismembering bodies. One young man, Carl Stottor, met Nilsen in the Mother Black

Cap. Back in Muswell Hill he survived Nilsen's attempts to strangle and then drown him, after which Nilsen walked him to the station. Nilsen was eventually caught after reporting blocked drains to Dynorod, whose engineer was surprised to discover that the problem was caused by human remains.

Behind Camden Road Station, No. 2 Ivor Street is less well known than Hilldrop Crescent, but it was the scene of equally gruesome events. Frank Hogg, a Kentish Town furniture mover, had two lovers – Mary Pearcey and Phoebe Styles. When Phoebe became pregnant, Frank moved in with her, and she soon had a daughter. Mary was furious and took her revenge. She invited Phoebe to her house at Ivor Street one Friday in October 1890, where she beat her to death with a poker and tried to cut her head off with a carving knife. She also killed the baby. Mary then wheeled the bodies in a pram a mile and half through Chalk Farm to a rubbish heap near Swiss Cottage, where she dumped them. When the police arrived at her blood-spattered house, she told them she had been dealing with a mouse problem. She was hanged for the murders, and subsequently featured as the only woman to be proposed as a Jack the Ripper candidate.

The turn of the century kept Edward Marshall Hall well employed, acting for Camden Town residents who found themselves in the Old Bailey. 'The Great Defender' had turned down the brief to defend Crippen when he refused to take Hall's advice, and was at the peak of his career when he came to defend Frederick Seddon in 1912. This time his rhetoric was in vain. Seddon, from Lancashire, was an insurance collector, second-hand clothes salesman, former preacher, Freemason and lover of money. He lived with his wife and five children at No. 63 Tollington Park near Finsbury Park, where he let rooms. In 1910, Eliza Barrow moved into one of them. She was a spinster with resources, including a large income from the Buck's Head pub on Camden High Street, which she owned. Her fortune included a cash box which may have contained as much as £150,000 in bags of gold.

By the following year Seddon had persuaded Barrow to sign over all her property and income to him, which he would look after in exchange for a rent-free room. Then Seddon's young daughter was sent out to buy flypaper which, in those days, contained arsenic. Barrow became sick with stomach pains, deteriorated over the course of six weeks, and died. Her suspicious relatives approached the police, who discovered that Barrow had been slowly poisoned with arsenic. Seddon's trial was undermined by his insistence on giving evidence, during which he offered a series of bizarre explanations for Barrow's death and talked himself onto the gallows. His final appeal to the judge as a fellow Freemason was declined, with regret, and Seddon became a popular waxwork in Madame Tussaud's Chamber of Horrors, alongside Mary Pearcey and Dr Crippen.

By the 1930s, Camden was established as a dirty and disreputable neighbourhood, the kind of place where people might well meet an unfortunate fate. In *Murder Underground*, a 1934 thriller by Mavis Doriel Hay, Miss Euphemia Pongleton is unable to keep her appointment with her dentist in Camden Town because she has been murdered. Her nephew Basil, investigating, complains about his dislike for 'the bus route past all the Camden Town fish shops' on Chalk Farm Road.[24] Meanwhile, in another 1934 crime novel, *A Pin to See the Peepshow* by Fryn Tennyson Jesse (great niece of Alfred), a character visits an address in Camden Town to arrange an illegal abortion – an indication of the way the neighbourhood was popularly viewed.

Behind the fish shops were the Regent's Canal back lands, occupied by small factories and wharves. A shed at the back of No. 30 Hawley Crescent was rented out as an office. Here, in 1934, a charred body was found slumped over an L. C. Smith & Corona typewriter. The shed had been doused with oil and deliberately set ablaze, but a typed sheet had mysteriously survived rolled inside the typewriter. It was a suicide note signed by Samuel Furnace, a thirty-nine-year-old builder with three children, claiming that money problems had led him to kill himself. The St Pancras coroner could understand neither the unburned note nor the unlikely self-immolation.

The body proved to be not Furnace, but that of a young rent collector called Walter Spatchett with three bullet holes in his back. Spatchett, a friend of Furnace who shared the office and had helped him financially in the past, had collected his day's rents and withdrawn savings. Now a sum of at least £40 and Samuel Furnace were missing. The latter was tracked down on the run in Southend, but he never made his trial. He had sewn a bottle of hydrochloric acid into his coat, which he drank in his cell at Kentish Town Police Station. He was found guilty post-mortem.

The Camden Ripper

In the summer of 2002, Camden became once again linked with murder. A violent decade in London peaked with eight separate, unrelated murders on the streets of Camden Town, Chalk Farm and Kentish Town between May and August, and an attempted drive-by shooting on Jamestown Road. The press began to use the term 'Murder Mile', previously reserved for Clapton, to refer to Camden High Street. Heroin and crack dealing had taken over the central Camden drug market, particularly on Inverness Street. 'There is a feeling of unease in Camden',[25] claimed local celebrity resident Jonathan Miller.

The unease was at its height when trainee rabbi Andreas Hinz met a man from Northern Ireland, Thomas McDowell, in the Mother Black Cap. McDowell lived in Cauldfield House on nearby Baynes Street, and was highly unstable. Hinz came back with him to the flat, where McDowell strangled him and cut up his body with a hacksaw. He placed the remains in a wheelie bin.

There was something in the air in Camden Town that year. McDowell was not the only person in the neighbourhood misusing Camden Council's bins. On the adjoining road, Royal College Street, Anthony Hardy occupied a one-bedroom council flat in a block called Hartland. He had spent years in mental hospitals, and was a large, intimidating man known to neighbours as 'The Bear'. In January 2002, the police visited Hardy's flat after a complaint that he had vandalised a neighbour's front door. In a locked room they found the body of his flatmate, Sally White. Despite evident injuries, the coroner found that she had died of natural causes. However, in December a tramp found the bodies of two women in wheelie bins on the corner of Hawley Crescent and Kentish Town Road. Further remains then showed up in another bin on Plender Street. Hardy went on the run, and was reported to have chatted amiably but persistently with unsuspecting women in central London parks. He was arrested at Great Ormond Street Hospital and eventually admitted to murdering two women, Bridgette MacClennan and Elizabeth Valad, as well as Sally White. He was sentenced to life, with the rare stipulation that he should never be released, after press coverage which labelled him 'The Camden Ripper'. McDowell, incarcerated in a secure hospital, was also recommended for a 'whole life' term.

The Regent's Canal, running through Camden Town like an open vein, is often the receptacle and transit point for unwanted goods. As a result, Camden has been the discovery sight for crimes committed upstream. John Sweeney, who described himself as 'The Scalp Hunter' received life, meaning life, after six holdalls were fished from the Regent's Canal and from a Rotterdam canal in 2001. He had killed two women while on the run from a jail sentence for attacking his girlfriend with an axe in Camden, in 1994. His Kentish Town flat was filled with hundreds of his paintings, showing women as demons. In July 2005, a carrier bag was found in the canal by a passer-by, filled with body parts. Marvin Gentles, a drug dealer, had been murdered by crack addict Abdul El-Gharras, who had stolen drugs given him to sell. Gentles came to his Lisson Grove flat, where El-Gharras stabbed him and cut him in small pieces with a saw. He then tried to cover his traces by setting fire to the flat.

The sombre start to the twenty-first century was a reminder that Camden Town remains a Victorian neighbourhood at heart, with one foot in the city of dreadful night. The undercurrent of threat and the unknown gives Camden its allure. Generally, despite the poverty, the crowds, the drink, the drugs and the rows, Camden remains in balance. When it tilts out of alignment, it reaches back to its pre-history as treacherous territory the traveller had no choice but to cross. From the World's End, journeys lead to unknown destinations.

The bridge over Regent's Canal at Hampstead Road Lock, 1909. Photograph by Alvin Langdon Coburn.

Chapter 2 **From Canal Town to Smoke Town, Gin Town, Piano Town and Market Town**

Camden Town owes its existence to the industrial age. While horses provided the only form of locomotion, the clay-heavy fields beyond St Pancras held no significance for anyone other than their few inhabitants. Once the Industrial Revolution began to gather momentum, rolling down from the north, Camden was transformed. It became a crucible for the new London. Goods travelled out on some of the earliest canals and railways in the capital, feeding an unstoppable demand for bodies. People arrived en masse to dig holes, feed furnaces and run engines, and their new houses packed the suddenly limited space, washing in waves around the new basins, yards, wharves, works and manufactories.

Camden Town came into being during the initial surge of London's great nineteenth-century growth. By the 1880s, a newly continuous city spread all the way from Chelsea to Hackney, and from Brixton up to the top of Haverstock Hill, surrounding Camden on all sides. London would was still growing and would not stop until the Second World War, but Camden was complete well before the nineteenth century was out. It has been shifting and adapting ever since, testing the constraints of its Victorian shape and coming to terms with the 'fiery eruptions' of its creation.[1] Aftershocks from the upheaval as the earth split apart giving birth to the train still ripple through Camden. Delving through layers of change helps to explain Camden as the product of its remarkable, industrial origins.

The Regent's Canal

From 1761, when coal first reached Manchester on the new Bridgewater Canal, artificial waterways quickly became the motorways of their age. The Grand Junction Canal of 1790 was conceived to link London directly to the already extensive canal networks of the Midlands and the North. A new web of canals was woven between the Thames and the western edges of London, creeping gradually closer to the city and terminating at Paddington in 1801, where the new basin was soon busy with everything from coal to household rubbish.

A plan to link Paddington Basin to the Thames became tied up with architect John Nash's super-sized development, sponsored by the Prince Regent, to build a grand boulevard from St James's Park all the way to the new Regent's Park. The latter was being laid out on land that had been Marylebone Farm, below Primrose Hill and next door to Camden, and it stood in the way of a canal extension. A speculator called Thomas Homer drew up plans for a new canal connection, but he made progress only when he took his ideas to Nash. The architect saw the canal as a suitable boundary, if diverted around the edge of his park, separating it from less socially aspirational districts beyond.

The first section of the Regent's Canal, from Paddington to Camden Town, opened in 1816 on the Prince Regent's birthday. It had taken four years to build, at a high cost. Four men were killed in an embankment collapse in Camden, and the repair bill came to more than the original budget for the entire canal. The long, curving route around the edge of Regent's Park also added to the expense, with seven separate bridges needed just to access the park. Thomas Homer, in severe debt, had been discovered embezzling canal funds. In 1815 he was given a seven-year sentence and transported to Australia.

Despite these problems, the remainder of the Regent's Canal opened in 1820, connecting Camden all the way to the new Limehouse Basin, and making it the gateway to the national canal system. The work was completed by men freshly available after the Battle of Waterloo, which had ended twenty years of gainful employment fighting Napoleon on the Continent. The canal connected the industrial heartlands to the Port of London and the world and, despite its financial problems, operated commercially for nearly 150 years. However, it was not long before the railways arrived in Camden to provide serious competition. In 1845 the Regent's Canal Company turned down an offer of £1 million to sell the canal for conversion to a railway line.

Camden's Locks

The famous stretch of canal that passes through the heart of Camden Town is not quite what it seems. There is, for a start, no Camden Lock. The name was invented by the founders of Lock Market, who saw it as more intuitive than the official name, Hampstead Road Lock. The canal setting for the market includes not one, but three lock systems within a few hundred yards. As well as Hampstead Road Lock, there are also Hawley and Kentish Town locks to the east, and together these slow down the narrowboats to supply a spectacle for gongoozling weekend crowds. They also attract all the detritus of the canal. There are no locks between Uxbridge and Camden, 26 miles away, so although the flow of water in the Regent's Canal is particularly slow at the Camden locks, everything that floats in the water upstream will eventually wash up in Camden.

Hampstead Road Lock was originally an experimental 'hydro-pneumatic' or caisson lock, invented in the late eighteenth century to reduce the huge volume of water lost every time a lock

View of Hampstead Lock, Camden.

is opened. The caisson lock used water pressure to seal barges in a chamber, which then passed underwater in a lift to the next level. The system, ingenious and terrifying in equal measure, was supposed to operate through natural buoyancy alone, with some versions designed to allow people to remain on board throughout.

The Hampstead Road Lock was a double version, allowing traffic in both directions at the same time. However, none of the caisson locks ever quite worked as intended. The Hampstead Road version required impossible amounts of strength to operate and was replaced by a more conventional double-lock in 1818. The diagonal Roving Bridge, which crosses at an angle between the Ice Wharf and the Lock Market, is part of the original design. It is diagonally aligned to give horses a better grip on the angled cobbles, which have nevertheless been polished smooth by passing hooves. The horses working the Lock were specially trained so that a slap on the flank from the tow-man would send them across the bridge on their own to take up position on the opposite bank, ready to pull barges heading back the other way.

Both narrowboats and barges (also known as lighters) were used on the Regent's Canal throughout its working life. While narrowboats are the classic canal craft still seen on the water, barges were larger, with sails so they could also transfer on to the Thames. The combined canal fleet delivered the materials that built Victorian London, loading up at the docks with goods such as imported timber from Norway, and bringing in goods from the furnaces and factories of Britain's industrial cities. Bricks, iron, timber and glass passed through the wharves of Camden, as well as coal to warm the new houses and fuel the factories.

The Hampstead Lock played a crucial role in John le Carré's cold war spy novel *Tinker, Tailor, Soldier, Spy*. The denouement, the unmasking of the high-ranking Soviet double agent within 'The Circus', is at a safe house in the fictional Five Lock Gardens: 'at the centre of a crescent, each with three floors and basement and a strip of walled back garden running down to the Regent's Canal'.[2] It is a low-key but respectable location with a wide selection of options for a quick getaway. The house is supposedly positioned beside the canal at the bottom of steps down from Gloucester Avenue, but there is no matching real-life location.

The Lost Market

The Regent's Canal had an extra branch, now lost, which continued around the eastern edge of Regent's Park. This was the half-mile long Cumberland Arm, which terminated at the Cumberland Basin. Today the lost canal can be detected at Gloucester Gate, where a bridge still crosses what are now gardens below. The Victorian bridge features a combined cattle trough and shrine to St Pancras, with a grotto and a highly androgynous statue. The saint reappears in a relief on the bridge, which shows him being mauled by a large dog. He looks as though he might be enjoying it.

The Cumberland Basin occupied a strange slice of London, at the edge of Camden, sandwiched between the palatial Nash houses facing Regent's Park and Euston Station. The basin was at the centre of a development built in the 1820s, which was designed as a new market centre for London. Three market squares were built – Cumberland Market for hay and straw, intended to replace the overcrowded Haymarket in the West End; Clarence Market for fruit and vegetables; and York Market, which never seems to have established a role for itself. The canal basin attracted factories and wharves, and by the late nineteenth century it was surrounded by timber and stone yards, piano manufacturers, a vinegar distillery, and two 'aerated water' factories.

The most famous building was the former Ophthalmic Hospital, designed by John Nash, where soldiers had been treated during the Napoleonic Wars. It was then used to manufacture the 'steam gun', a steam-powered machine cannon designed by Jacob Perkins, who also invented the first modern refrigeration system. The cannon was demonstrated to the Dukes of Sussex and Wellington, and the latter is reported to have thought it 'Damn'd wonderful! Damn'd wonderful!'[3] However, the Army was less keen and the venture was a failure. The factory was then taken on by Cornish steam pioneer Sir Goldsworthy Gurney, who manufactured the steam carriage, a steam-driven road vehicle which he tested in the factory yard and on local roads at reckless speeds of up to 20 miles per hour. Finally, the former hospital became a distillery for Booth's gin, which was closed at the end of the nineteenth century in favour of its better known premises at Farringdon.

Cumberland Basin was also the site of London's first ice well, which consisted of a brick-lined chamber 80 feet deep with a drain dug through the London clay to the chalk, 300 feet below. It was built in 1825 by William Leftwich, who started out selling ice that was skimmed from the Regent's Canal. He later graduated to imported Norwegian ice, brought to Limehouse by sea and shipped up the canal. The business expanded to new wells in the 1830s, building two more, 100 feet deep, at Ice Wharf on the south side of Camden Lock. The well at Cumberland Basin was filled when Cumberland Market was rebuilt after the Second World War, and the Camden Lock wells are preserved under flats that were built on the site in the 2000s.

Although the canal basin was relatively well used, the markets were essentially a failure and never attracted the anticipated business. The poet Charlotte Mew described it as 'a place of carts and the sky. Cabs and trains know nothing of it'.[4] The Cumberland Market neighbourhood has always been oddly hidden away. York Market became Munster Square, and Clarence Market was turned into a garden. By the early twentieth century the neighbourhood was run-down, providing the cheap accommodation used by, among others, the Cumberland Market artists (discussed in Chapter 4). By 1930 the canal basin had closed and only one pub remained open. Demolition and rebuilding began in 1938, when the basin was drained, and continued during the Blitz when it was filled with rubble from bombed buildings.

The rest of the area, badly bomb-damaged, was completely redeveloped after the war as the Regent's Park Estate. A self-contained district of modernist council blocks, many named after Lake District locations, it is probably the least known and least visited part of Camden, often not seen as related to Camden Town at all. The neighbourhood, sometimes described as West Euston, has liminal qualities, falling between Regent's Park, Camden Town and Euston where it floats, as though only semi-visible. Buried deep among the hidden courtyards, pedestrian cut-throughs and blind alleys of the Regent's Park Estate are the concealed allotments that now occupy the site of the lost canal basin.

This combination of centrality and obscurity suits the more specialised branches of the military. Tucked discreetly between the park and the railway lines, Regent's Park Barracks is home to the SAS. The regiment headquartered here is 21 SAS, which began life in 1859 as the Artist's Rifles, founded during a scare over war with France, to encourage painters, sculptors, architects and other creative types to join up. Today it covers the southern half of Britain, as well as deployments overseas. The north is covered by 23 SAS (based in Birmingham), and between them the two regiments are reported to have responsibility for 'countering domestic subversion'.

The Railways Come to Camden

The capital's first railway terminus, London Bridge Station, opened in 1836. The following year, as the first railway boom took off, the London and Birmingham Railway (L&BR) opened its line to Euston. It passed straight through Camden, which still consisted of little more than a grid of nine streets, only partly filled with houses. Until the railway arrived, Camden was as much rural as it was urban. The process of change that followed, involving transformation on a scale that had barely been witnessed before, anywhere, came to define the time and the place.

Camden gave Charles Dickens his first experience of London. His parents moved to No. 16 Bayham Street from Chatham in

Building the Retaining Walls Near Park Street, Camden Town, September 15th 1836. Print by J. C. Bourne. This scene shows the Camden section of the construction of the London to Birmingham railway, which was completed in 1838.

1822, and the young Charles first saw urban poverty in newly developed Camden. His nineteenth-century biographer reports that 'Bayham Street was then about the poorest part of the London suburbs, and the house was a mean, small tenement, with a wretched little garden abutting on a squalid court'.[5] Camden was still a village and 'Bayham Street had grass struggling through the newly paved road'.[6] There was no street lighting, but there was a cabin in the gardens of the Mother Red Cap which housed the village watchman. Dickens's father, John, walked across the fields into London for his job at Somerset House. In 1824, with his father imprisoned for debt, Dickens lodged briefly at No. 112 College Place while working in a shoe-blacking factory near Charing Cross. Later, coincidentally, the wood engravings by Chapman & Hall that illustrated his novels were produced by the Camden Press, a family firm run by the Dalziel brothers, based at a Bayham Street workshop accessed through an arch from No. 110 Camden High Street. The Dalziels were London's engravers of choice, supplying illustrations for the novels and the popular press of the nineteenth century, such as the *Illustrated London News*.

No. 16 Bayham Street was demolished in 1910, but survives in the descriptions of the Micawbers' house in *David Copperfield* and the Cratchit family house in *A Christmas Carol*, both explicitly located in the modest surroundings of Camden Town. The Camden description for which Dickens is best remembered, though, is from *Dombey and Son*. Published in 1848, it includes a famous, typically flamboyant account of the construction of the L&BR:

> The first shock of a great earthquake had, just at that period, rent the whole neighbourhood to its centre. Traces of its course were visible on every side. Houses were knocked down; streets broken through and stopped; deep pits and trenches dug in the ground; enormous heaps of earth and clay thrown up; buildings that were undermined and shaking, propped by great beams of wood. Here, a chaos of carts, overthrown and jumbled together, lay topsy-turvy at the bottom of a steep unnatural hill; there, confused treasures of iron soaked and

rusted in something that had accidentally become a pond. Everywhere were bridges that led nowhere; thoroughfares that were wholly impassable; Babel towers of chimneys, wanting half their height; temporary wooden houses and enclosures, in the most unlikely situations; carcases of ragged tenements, and fragments of unfinished walls and arches, and piles of scaffolding, and wildernesses of bricks, and giant forms of cranes, and tripods straddling above nothing. There were a hundred thousand shapes and substances of incompleteness, wildly mingled out of their places, upside down, burrowing in the earth, aspiring in the air, mouldering in the water, and unintelligible as any dream. Hot springs and fiery eruptions, the usual attendants upon earthquakes, lent their contributions of confusion to the scene. Boiling water hissed and heaved within dilapidated walls; whence, also, the glare and roar of flames came issuing forth; and mounds of ashes blocked up rights of way, and wholly changed the law and custom of the neighbourhood. In short, the yet unfinished and unopened Railroad was in progress.[7]

Dickens was not averse to a little exaggeration for effect, but the new railway drove a vast trench from Primrose Hill to Euston which remains in place today, comprehensively separating Camden from its wealthier neighbours to the west in Regent's Park. The transformation was deep and long-lasting, lifting Camden Town out of obscurity and dropping it into a crucial junction in the transport network. Railway pioneer Robert Stephenson was in charge of bringing the railway to London from Birmingham, and the purchase of land at Camden was his project. Camden was originally planned as the terminus for the new line, but the L&BR came to realise that a station was needed closer to the centre, and paid for extra land at Euston. This final stretch of line proved problematic. In the early days the steep gradient, created because the line had to duck under the Regent's Canal, meant that locomotives had to be hauled to Camden from Euston Station up the Camden Incline. A steam-powered winding house was built by the canal, with a pair of tall slim chimneys as landmarks, either side of the line. By 1844 locomotives had become more powerful, and two working together could handle the slope, so the engines were dismantled and sold to a flax mill in Russia.

Shortly after the line opened, a new goods depot was established on Lord Southampton's land between the railway and Chalk Farm Road, then called Pancras Vale. The North London line opened in the 1850s, meeting the Euston main line at the Camden depot site. It linked Camden to the West India Docks, with the now lost Primrose Hill Station north of the Roundhouse on Regent's Park Road, giving Camden's railways the same reach as the canal. The railway company, now the London and North Western Railway (L&NWR), moved all its goods activities to the new depot, which soon took up a large slice of north Camden and became known as Camden Goods Station. A 2,000 foot-long brick boundary wall was built along Pancras Vale in the 1850s, to hold in the huge volumes of tunnel spoil deposited on the site as foundations.

Railway Town

Camden Goods Station covered a site more than 30 acres in size, which became a citadel of transport and industry. As well as the Roundhouse, a collection of distinctive, multi-storey brick warehouses sprang up among the sidings served by a network of tunnels. The depot handled livestock when first built, with cattle pens from which beasts were driven through the streets to Smithfield. This practice ended when the new, super-modern Metropolitan Cattle Market opened on Caledonian Road in 1854, but the Goods Station still had more animals than machines. The L&NWR made extensive provisions for the small army of horses and ponies that not only hauled goods around the site, but also shunted goods wagons, and carried on doing so until the late nineteenth century. Horses were originally stabled in vaults under the sidings, many of which survive today in the Stables Market and the Horse Tunnel Market, the entrance to the latter marked with an oddly glamorous relief sculpture of horses, manes flying, emerging from the surf. By 1849 the extended vaults housed over 400 horses. Between the 1850s and the 1880s four more stable blocks and a Horse Hospital were added, creating the complex that now houses the Stables Market. The Horse Hospital has a specially built horse ramp, known as a horse creep, which is now the northern exit from the market, and there used to be another on the west side of what is now Dingwall's.

The stables were connected under the railway lines by two separate horse tunnels, built so horses would not need to cross the tracks. The Eastern Horse Tunnel connected the Interchange Warehouse, now occupied by the head office of the Associated Press. The tunnel exit via special 'horse stairs' is fenced and covered, but can still be seen beside Henson House next door. The yard outside has grilles in the cobbles to ventilate and light the space below. The Western Horse Tunnel passes under the main line to Euston on the west side of the market, with horse stairs at the end of what is now Gilbey's Yard, and an exit at the other end which is now part of a restaurant on Gloucester Avenue.

This tunnel and vault complex is known as the Camden Town Catacombs, and forms an extensive, crypt-like series of brick spaces similar to those found under London Bridge or Waterloo Stations. The building of the New Market Hall in the 1980s closed off part of the network, which also had connections into the basements of now-demolished warehouses. However, as well as the Stables and Horse Tunnel Markets, two hidden areas of vaulting remain intact. One vaults lies under the yard outside the Interchange Building, between the canal and the market, and under No. 30 Oval Road, next door. The Stephenson Vaults are below the Euston main line, under the site of the engines that once pulled trains up the Camden Incline, linked via the Western Horse Tunnel. These underground spaces are all infamously difficult to access, but there are now plans in the ether to open and develop some of these spaces.

The Catacombs are also connected to an underground canal dock, the Interchange Basin, better known as Dead Dog Basin. An opening in the canal wall, cheerfully known as Dead Dog Hole, gives boats access to the basin which is hidden under the

The Eastern Horse Tunnel, Camden Town Catacombs, 1987. Photograph by Nick Catford.

Interchange Warehouse. Built around 1905, the warehouse was used to transfer loads between Thames barges, narrowboats, goods trains and carts. It originally also had direct access for trains, with railway lines running all the way through the building to the canal. Basement arches contained bonded warehouses (secure storage where goods are kept before customs duty is paid) that were used to store Gilbey's gin, as well as potatoes and fodder.

Gin Town

Furniture removal firm Pickfords were early tenants at the Goods Station. They moved from City Basin in 1841, building a state-of-the-art warehouse on Jamestown Road, with barge access in the basement and railway access to the ground floor, via private bridges over the canal. This burned down in a spectacular fire in 1857, but was rebuilt at even greater expense, becoming supposedly the largest warehouse on the railway system.

The firm most closely linked to Camden was W. & A. Gilbey – one of the five main producers of London gin (with Beefeater, Booth's, Gordon's and Nicholson's). The 'W' stood for Walter and the 'A' for Alfred. The two brothers found themselves in need of employment on being discharged at the end of the Crimean War in 1856. Joining up with a third brother, Henry, a wine merchant, they became very successful importing French wines. They were based at the Pantheon, a former exhibition hall on Oxford Street (the Gilbey headquarters until 1937).

They moved into gin in 1872, setting up their distillery on Oval Road in a building that had been Camden Flour Mills. The company became a wines and spirits behemoth, importing sparkling wines, sherry and rum, and by the early twentieth century they owned dozens of Scottish and Irish whisky distilleries. American Prohibition was a boom time for the company. A team of women was employed to sew cases of gin and whisky into unlabelled sacks. Having first been shipped to Amsterdam, the

View of the despatching floor at W. & A. Gilbey, in the Right Hon. Sir Herbert Maxwell, *W. Gilbey and [A.] Ltd, Half-a-century of Successful Trade: Being a Sketch of the Rise and Development of the Business of W. & A. Gilbey. 1857–1907.* Printed for private circulation, 1907.

sacks eventually reached the States via rowing boats, and were unloaded on the Eastern Seaboard under cover of darkness.

Camden became Gilbey's main location, and the firm expanded across the Goods Station site. The enormous 'A' Shed, on the opposite side of Oval Road from the distillery, was linked under the road by a series of tunnels and had its own railway connection across the canal. The drink was held in bonded warehouses at the Goods Station, controlled by customs officials who levied duty on everything that left the buildings. The Interchange Warehouse became No. 1 Bond, the Roundhouse became No. 3 Bond (holding fifteen vast vats of maturing whisky), while Nos 2 and 4 Bond were on the Chalk Farm Road side of the site. What remains of them is now part of the Stables Market. Gilbey's influence spread all the way across Camden Town, with No. 5 Bond located in the railway arches some distance away at Camden Road Station.

The distinctive Gilbey's buildings, converted to other uses, still shape the south side of the canal. The 'A' Shed now contains flats and the offices of comedy producers, Hat Trick. The most impressive remnant of Gilbey's reign, on the corner of Jamestown Road and Oval Road, is Gilbey House. It was built in 1937 as new offices for the firm, replacing the Stanhope Arms pub which stood on the corner with Gilbey's distillery wrapped around it. The new building, then called Academic House, had white-washed walls, stark geometry, and deep, round skylights punched through the roof. These tell-tale signs betray the work of modernist architect Serge Chermayeff, who also designed the more celebrated De La Warr Pavilion in Bexhill-on-Sea, East Sussex, with Erich Mendelsohn. The building, which originally had 'Gilbey' spelled from top to bottom in giant, 1930s chrome lettering, still looks eerily modern. Meanwhile, the triangular Bottle Stores, where bottles were washed and packed, burned down in 1980 (the Gilgamesh building and New Market Hall now occupy the site).

However, gin was not the only drink for which Camden would become known. A Welsh chemist called Thomas Howell Williams

View of the exterior of Gilbey House in 1937.

opened a mineral water factory on Pratt Street in 1873. His business, which drew its water from deep below Camden via an artesian well, was called Idris & Co after Cader Idris, the mountain of Welsh legend that sits high above Aberystwyth. The business was a success, producing ginger beer, lemonade and soda water, as well as less familiar concoctions such as Phosphade and Koolime. The proprietor, who later changed his name to Thomas Howell Idris, served as Mayor of St Pancras and then as a Liberal MP in Wales. Idris & Co continued producing fizzy drinks in Camden until 1965, also bottling 7-Up and Coca-Cola. The firm moved to a new factory in Tottenham, and was bought by Beecham and then by Britvic, but Idris Fiery Ginger Beer remains widely available.

Smoke Town

The Goods Station turned Camden into an unmistakably industrial neighbourhood. Smoke from the engines deposited endless soot over the streets closest to the railway lines. The west side of Camden became grubby, the houses occupied by railway workers and navvies, and brothels were reported by the police in streets in Primrose Hill and between Regent's Park and the railway.

H. G. Wells lived at No. 46 Fitzroy Road, Primrose Hill, from 1889 to 1891, where he complained about the noise and the smoke from passing trains. The Martian invaders in his science-fiction novel *The War of the Worlds* set up camp on Primrose Hill, and Christopher Rolfe suggests that the 'Martian fighting machines, described by one witness as boilers on stilts, were inspired by those engines belching fire and sooty smoke'.[8] Wells was also attuned to the workings of the London and North Western Railway, describing scenes of panic on Chalk Farm Road as crowds struggle to escape on the L&NWR trains (which, in his novel, have been forced to terminate at Camden Goods Station rather than at Euston).

The railway pall still hung over post-war Camden in the 1950s, with 'The whole street bathed in smoke for much of the day;

indoors was the grime of the corrosive dust that spread from the sidings and the main line'.[9] Primrose Hill Primary, known as 'The Smoke School', was next to the coaling station where engines queued, pumping black smoke into the air. Resident Caroline Ramsden noted that 'The dirt which collected everywhere had to be encountered to be believed'.[10] There was great relief when the railway line was electrified in 1960. However, as in much of London, 150 years of soot took a long time to disappear.

The white stucco houses of Mornington Terrace, overlooking the railway, were still soot-blackened in the 1980s, and the massive retaining wall running the length of Chalk Farm Road (known as the Great Wall of Camden) was stained, dark and forbidding before it was eventually cleaned (and partially demolished) for the development of the Goods Station site. David Thomson wrote of his aversion to the blackened Chalk Farm Road 'prison wall', which locked the entire street in perpetual shadow.[11] However, the railway also provided inspiration. Filmmaker Humphrey Jennings lived on Regent's Park Terrace, closed to the main line cutting. Co-founder of the social research project 'Mass Observation', and famed for wartime documentaries such as *Fires Were Started*, Jennings loved the railways. His masterwork, *Pandaemonium*, an anthology of contemporary accounts of the coming of the machine to Britain, includes an entire section on the railways.

Piano Town

Camden's late nineteenth-century industrial reputation was not confined to gin and locomotives. There was manufacturing of many kinds taking place all over the neighbourhood – metal casting in Bayham Street; engineering on Pratt Street; playing card and stationery manufacturing on Royal College Street; printing on Camden Street; brewing at the Elephant Brewery on Hawley Street, and wharves running the length of the canal, bringing materials in and taking goods out. However, Camden was once known above all for a particular industry.

Until the First World War, Camden Town was the piano-making centre of Britain. If there seems to be a large number of converted buildings called 'The Piano Factory' or similar, it is because nearly all the piano manufacturers in Britain were once based in Camden and Islington. At the start of the twentieth century, over 120 firms could be found in Camden Town, including once famous, now forgotten, companies such as Gunther & Horwood, J. J. Hopkinson and George Rogers & Sons. Camden was an ideal centre for collecting raw materials and transporting finished products, via canal and rail, to Britain and the Empire.

The piano was in fact first demonstrated in Britain by a Camden resident – musical celebrity Charles Dibdin, who lived in Arlington Road. He was known for his patriotic sea-shanties, popular during the Napoleonic Wars, and for topical musical 'entertainments' with titles such as *The General Election* and *Great News – A Trip to the Antipodes*. These have not lasted, but his shanty 'Tom Bowling' is still sung at the Last Night of the Proms. In 1765, during scene changes between acts of *The Beggar's Opera* at Covent Garden, he broke new ground by entertaining the audience with songs accompanied by a Miss Bricklet at 'the new pianoforte'. A Celtic cross in St Martin's Gardens, Camden Street, replaces his original tomb which collapsed. His epitaph is from 'Tom Bowling': 'His form was of the manliest beauty, His heart was kind and soft, Faithful, below, he did his duty; But now he's gone aloft.'

The best remaining example of Camden's piano days is the Collard & Collard building on Oval Road, at the corner of Gloucester Crescent. The Oval factory was in fact round, built with large windows flooding circular workshops with light. Collard & Collard moved out in the 1920s (although only as far as Chalk Farm Road), as German pianos took over the market. The rotunda still stands, and has since housed various businesses including pioneering publisher of women authors, Virago Press. When

Collard & Collard occupied the site, it was the hub of an industry that dominated the area. Pianos are complex machines, requiring many speciality parts, and these were all made in Camden. Nearby workshops produced components from ivory piano keys and hammer felts, to castors and the candle sconces for lighting the music. Pianoforte smallwork makers carved the screens, and pianoforte silkers made the back cloths. Marquetry cutters, carvers, gilders and French polishers turned pianos into decorative objects. Then there were piano storage warehouses, piano movers, piano tuners and piano galleries, and piano teachers or, in more upmarket Gloucester Crescent, professors of music and singing. Camden was piano town.

Nor was Camden just concerned with pianos. Humphrey's American Organ Factory was based on Little Camden Street (now Mandela Street), but perhaps the most famous firm was found in another rotunda at the north end of Royal College Street, where Camden shades into Kentish Town. Subsequently occupied by Richard of Chichester School, and now flats, this was the location of 'Father' Henry Willis's organ factory, set up in 1865. Willis founded the firm that built the world's largest symphonic organs for High Victorian settings, among them the Great Exhibition, the Royal Albert Hall and Windsor Castle. His firm equipped the grand houses, town halls and churches of Britain with teetering stacks of silvered pipework and polished mahogany. Willis organs can still be found in cathedrals from Carlisle to Calcutta, concert halls from Brighton to Brisbane, and across London from the heights of Alexandra Palace to King's College Chapel, off the Strand. Henry Willis & Sons moved out of Camden in 1908, but the firm continues to operate from a factory in Liverpool called the Rotunda Works.

The invention of recorded music eventually put paid to the piano as a standard household object, but traces of the industry linger. Until 1998, Herrburger Brooks ran a factory at No. 31 Lyme Street, where they were the world's oldest manufacturer of piano mechanisms and keyboards. One of the last piano firms in

Camden was Hecksher's. In 2014 it closed its piano restoration shop on Bayham Street, where it had opened at the height of the piano boom in 1883. However, at least two piano businesses remain in Camden, with distinctly contrasting styles. Camden Piano Rescue in the Lock Market carries out restoration from a converted workshop above the stalls, while Markson's on Albany Street, beside the Regent's Park Estate, has a grand showroom full of Bechsteins and a pedigree to match.

Camden in the Round

Camden had, at one time, four rotundas – the Roundhouse, the Collard & Collard rotunda, the Willis & Sons rotunda and the Colosseum, on the fringes of Camden next to Regent's Park.

The Kentish Town Rotunda, later home to Henry Willis & Sons, owes its shape to its original function. It was built in 1824 to house a giant panoramic painting. These were enormously popular attractions in the early nineteenth century. Vast, 360-degree cycloramic paintings of views, battles, disasters and spectacles were exhibited to the public, for a fee, in specially designed buildings. The most famous was the Leicester Square Panorama, but the Kentish Town Rotunda contained a copy of a spectacular view of London that had been painted from the top of St Paul's Cathedral by Thomas Hornor. He had worked on his sketches early in the morning, before smoke from the fires of the city blotted out the view, working in a purpose-built shack precariously nested in scaffolding over the golden orb and cross, at the very top of the cathedral dome. The Kentish Town Rotunda was later taken over by a painter called Robert Burford, who used it as a workshop for painting panoramas which he supplied to Leicester Square.

The Kentish Town Rotunda was just the beginning for Hornor, who moved on to a much more ambitious venture across Camden – the London Colosseum (which was based, in fact,

Engraving showing the Colosseum in 1827, with a view of the Grand Panorma of London as an inset in the foreground. George Walter Thornbury, *Old and New London*, Cassell & Co., 1887–93.

on the Pantheon in Rome). It was purpose-built to display the Grand Panorama of London, a larger version of Hornor's London cyclorama. The work was painted, scaled-up, on the walls and ceiling of the Colosseum by a team led by the artist E. T. Parris, who did much of the job perilously suspended from the ceiling.

The Colosseum was an extravagant and unlikely building. It was designed by Decimus Burton, also responsible for laying out Hyde Park, and consisted of a Classical portico attached to the front of a vast, glass-domed cylinder. The whole structure looked like an early gasholder. It included the world's first passenger lift – 'an Ascending Room, raised by secret machinery' – invented to transport visitors to viewing level. Hornor completed the project at enormous expense, with the help of financial backers including an MP called Rowland Stephenson. The Colosseum opened in 1827, but both Hornor and Stephenson fled the country a year later. Stephenson, who was reported to have removed hundreds of thousands of bonds from the firm where he worked and bought himself a pair of pistols, resurfaced in Savannah, Georgia. He was caught in New York by bounty hunters, but managed to avoid deportation. Soon, however, he was in jail in Virginia over new debts he had run up there. Hornor ended up in New York too, where he died, penniless, in 1844.

The Colosseum, remarkably, survived. Trustees took over the business, and the show was remodelled in 1843 with a new Grand Panorama, and other attractions including a Swiss cottage with views of 'real' waterfalls and the Glyptotheka, a pseudo-Classical sculpture museum. The lift was given an Elizabethan makeover. Later, an after-dark panorama of the great 1755 Lisbon Earthquake was added, but by then the panorama fashion was truly over, and the Colosseum lingered unused until it was demolished in 1874. It was replaced by the Cambridge Gate blocks of flats, next to the Royal College of Physicians, which overlooks Regent's Park.

Motorway Malaise

After the Second World War, Camden Town, in common with the rest of industrial central London, entered a prolonged slump as de-industrialisation tightened its grip and many people moved out of town. Some areas would need fifty years and more to recover, although Camden managed a head start, later leading the revival of inner London. Camden Town had been heavily bombed, with considerable destruction in the area north of Camden Town Underground Station, which itself took a direct hit. In Harrington Square, where trenches had been dug before the war during the 1938 Munich Crisis, a raid killed eleven people and left a double-decker bus in a crater. However, the Camden goods yards were relatively unscathed, and the Gilbey's buildings on the north side of the canal survived intact. They were to form the base on which Camden's future would eventually be constructed. However, things would get worse before they began to get better.

The winter of 1962/63, known as the Big Freeze, was the worst of the century, and is often blamed for finishing off the commercial canal system in Britain. As the country's waterways froze and stayed frozen for two months, traffic did indeed come to a halt. Barges with coal for power stations were immobilised, supplies could not be delivered and business transferred to road haulage firms. Some barges never moved again, with two scuttled in one of the Dingwall's wharves and then entombed in concrete under the West Yard. However, the railways and roads had similar problems with the weather, and the story is not as clear-cut as subsequently made out. The canal system was already in decline for various reasons, competition from road transport being one, and the Big Freeze just made things worse.

The Regent's Canal eventually closed to shipping in 1969, and lay run-down for several years afterwards with its towpaths closed to the public. However, although run-down and bomb-damaged, Camden had already begun to use the canal differently. The first pleasure boat on the Regent's Canal was licensed in 1951, and by the mid-1960s an industry had grown up. School children took trips to London Zoo on narrowboats from Camden.

By this time Camden had become embroiled in the notorious London Motorway Box scheme. Collectively known as the London Ringways, this comprehensive inner ring-road plan had its origins in a 1938 report co-authored by Sir Edwin Lutyens, better known for designing New Delhi. Sir Patrick Abercrombie, architect and town planner for the post-Second World War reconstruction of London, included in his plans a long-term scheme to construct an inner and an outer ring road for Greater London. By the early 1960s plans had mutated into a colossal proposal to build a system of four 'ringways'. Of these, Ringway 2 eventually became the North Circular Road, and Ringways 3 and 4 the M25.

The inner route, Ringway 1 (or the Motorway Box), was only ever partially built. It would have carved its way across North London, taking the route of the canal through Camden Town. The Westway would have extended along the canal route all the way through Camden, where there would have been two junctions – a motorway spur to Euston from Camden Lock, and another spur to the North Circular Road from Camden Road. The two sections of the Motorway Box that were eventually built (the Westway, and the West Cross Route and the East Cross Route) were destructive and wildly unpopular, and have blighted their neighbourhoods ever since. They show exactly what would have happened to Camden Town had the scheme gone ahead.

Fortunately, opposition was organised and determined, and the plans proved too destructive even for the time. The scheme was cancelled in 1973. However, it had left central Camden in limbo for a decade, waiting for its future to be determined. In the meantime, industries had moved out and space lay unclaimed. In 1962, the family-owned W. & A. Gilbey was bought by United Wine Traders, and became International Distillers and Vintners. The new conglomerate moved to a new plant in Harlow, part of the tide of heavy industry leaving inner London. After nearly a hundred years dominating Camden, both physically and economically, Gilbey's was gone, leaving acres of disused buildings behind.

The railways were also moving out. Behind the Great Wall of Camden, which still ran unbroken along the entire west side of Chalk Farm Road, the Goods Yard was abandoned as transport moved to the roads. The place that had provided the rationale for Camden Town from the very beginning lay empty, and a new rationale was needed.

The two parts of the site were treated very differently. While the former Gilbey buildings on the south side of the canal underwent a startling transformation to become the Lock Market, the north of the Goods Station site was redeveloped in the early 1990s in particularly uninspiring fashion. A long stretch of the Great Wall was demolished and a tunnel built under the railway to reach a large, out-of-town style supermarket (now Morrisons), with an even larger car park. Two sets of housing were also built – a street called Gilbey's Yard and Juniper Crescent, a strange island squeezed between the two railway lines. The development revealed that the Goods Station sat on a layer of ashes and spoil eight metres deep, most of which had to be dug out. The North London line and the main line to Euston still cross the site, but otherwise railway operations ended here in 1992 when Primrose Hill Station, behind the Roundhouse, closed. Discussions were underway at the time of writing to redevelop the Morrisons site to give much-needed character back to Camden's deadest zone.

Market Town

At the heart of Camden, a green railway bridge announces 'Camden Lock' in yellow, barge art lettering. The largest street market in the country is right here but, despite its name being as well-known as Oxford Street, there is no Camden Market as such. There are several different markets clustered around the canal bridge and strung along Camden High Street and Chalk Farm

Road. The place that most people think of as Camden Market is actually two intertwined markets, hard to tell apart – the Lock Market and the Stables Market. The original market is Camden Lock Market, sprawling in and around a set of warehouses that belonged to a timber wharf, and were originally part of the Goods Station. Further up the Chalk Farm Road, behind a long wall, is the Stables Market. Next to Camden Town tube, Buck Street Market squeezes on to a triangular site, while Inverness Street Market, off the High Street, has a road to itself. Over the road from the Lock, between the railway and Hawley Wharf, the Canal Street Market burned down in 2008 and is the site of a major rebuild. In addition, Camden High Street itself is a market between the Lock and Camden Town tube station.

The idea of Camden as a marketplace is not new. In 1878 Edward Walford wrote of Camden High Street that 'On Saturday evenings the upper part of the street, thronged as it is with stalls of itinerant vendors of the necessaries of daily life, and with the dwellers in the surrounding districts, presents to an ordinary spectator all the attributes of a market place'.[12] Inverness Street Market has a long pedigree as an everyday produce market, although its fruit and veg stalls closed during the 2000s.

The Lock Market was founded by Bill Fulford and Peter Wheeler, two young developers who had begun by converting Clapham houses into flats. After scouting around the London docks, they were tipped off about the T. E. Dingwall timber yard in Camden. In 1937 the T. E. Dingwall firm had leased the central stable block at Purfleet Wharf, previously used to store Anglo-American Oil drums, as a timber yard. Here the firm offloaded timber from canal barges and used it to make packing cases.

The Dingwall family decided to sell up in 1971 and, to their credit, were attracted by Fulford and Wheeler's plans to do something different with the site. At first the developers could only get temporary planning permission to change the use of the timber yard, because it was still theoretically reserved for a motorway. Nevertheless, they were allowed to open workshops, restaurants and a snack bar, and an office. Although the market's founders now spend their time elsewhere, in Fulford's case as a university professor, their company Northside Developments still part-owns the market.

The Dingwall site had three yards – East, Middle and West – which became the secret of the Lock Market's success. The connected, self-contained spaces are all different and, along with the system of strangely labyrinthine passageways that lead into the Stables Market, turn the whole place into an adventure. Craft units were made available in the East Yard and were taken up by artists, many fresh out of college, and a wide range of craftspeople. They sold painted bargeware, old fairground equipment, sculptures made from cutlery. There were cartoonists, a blacksmith, toymakers, furniture makers, jewellers (Five Jewellers), window blinds (Blind Alley) and waterbeds (Cloud Nine). Market manager Eric Reynolds built racing yachts by day in the corrugated iron-roofed Black Sheds, winching them up to the roof to make way for stalls at weekends.

The antiques market, which opened in the East Yard in 1974, set the scene for Camden. Stall holders selling unusual wares – Afghan carpets, Peruvian knitwear, eccentric bric-a-brac – were actively encouraged, and the market quickly became popular. Stalls were allocated by lottery. The Lock Shop, a corrugated iron shed painted with clouds and rainbows, sold bespoke crafts and clothing. Among the hippy-heaven vibes, there were also two relatively high-end restaurants which attracted people with money to spend, such as Paul McCartney.

Before long, the market also became known for its niche fashions – mod, rocker and skinhead gear – and the hippy atmosphere dissipated as punk broke into Camden. Joe Strummer and Topper Headon of the Clash, and Dave Stewart and Annie Lennox of the Tourists (later to become the Eurythmics), all ran short-term stalls on the market to fund their musical ambitions.

Meanwhile, Dingwall's Dance Hall opened in 1973, soon after the Wharf was converted from the Dingwall packaging warehouse.

View of Camden Lock market with Dingwall's club, taken in 1976.

It staged bands every night and jazz Saturday lunchtimes, with a bar that also sold food, which was enough to bring in an arty crowd usually found only in Soho – David Hockney, Lucian Freud, George Melly, David Gilmour of Pink Floyd. It even sold good beer, which in the early 1970s was Adnams. It was, however, run on the cheap, so the toilets were terrible and the whole place had a reputation for smelling bad. Co-owner Tony Mackintosh said, 'When it was good it was absolutely fabulous, when it was bad it was dreadful'.[13] By 1974 the Stranglers were referring to 'Dingwall's bullshit' in their song 'London Lady', and the venue was established as the place to go.

Not everything was new and creative though. The 'Camden criminal fraternity' kept a close eye on the market, taking a particular interest in the showground wagon, parked in the Middle Yard, where artist Wilf Scott lived. As it turned out their interest was not entirely selfless. Scott reported that 'One night there was a bang on my wagon and this man said "Let me in, I've got to hide here because I just murdered someone". He was big so I let him in'.[14]

By the time Ringway 1 was cancelled, the temporary market leases at Dingwall's Wharf were up, and immediately commercial and creative considerations collided. British Waterways wanted to redevelop the site, and the work Northside Developments had done on setting up the craft workshops gave them the first claim to lead the plans. The first plan from Col. Richard Seifert, designer of Centrepoint and almost every other tall London building of the time, was to knock everything down: 'That's what you did back then', claimed Fulford. Seifert's scheme was rejected, as were subsequent proposals.

For a few years the rebuilding of the Lock Market stalled. However, Seifert's firm did rebuild a lock cottage on Oval Road in 1977 as the Pirate Castle, the headquarters of the Pirate Club, a canoeing and rowing charity for the young people of canal-side Camden. A pumping station opposite, built in 1980 in the same piratey style, uses canal water to cool mains electricity cables under the towpath.

In 1983 the Railway Tavern on Chalk Farm Road changed its name to the Lock Tavern, a symbolic shift. The long-postponed market redevelopment finally began when the New Market Hall was built on the East Yard. In 1980 the first of two 'Fires of Camden' had destroyed Gilbey's Bottle Store, the four-storey triangular warehouse at the centre of the market, next to the railway bridge. It had been used for storing furniture and burned so fiercely that it entirely collapsed. The site remained derelict for more than a decade, eventually being redeveloped with a glass-fronted corner section occupied by novelty restaurant Gilgamesh. The New Market Hall development, built on the east side of the market in 1991, was designed to mimic the nineteenth-century railway buildings. These redevelopments changed the market, chasing out many of the original book and antique dealers and craftspeople. Although a small number remain, the Lock Market is no longer the craft centre that formed the basis of the original market.

The name Camden Lock came out of a rebranding exercise, during which the market just escaped becoming 'King Camden'. The owners rightly noted that the Hampstead Road Lock was not on Hampstead Road, and the market needed to be more direct. The market was actively promoted in other ways during the 1980s, using street performance such as fire-eating and juggling, and events such as the Festival of Clocks. This type of entertainment, which now sounds very much of its time, is still closely associated with Covent Garden Market, redeveloped around the same time.

However, the market was still an alternative destination. Camden and Kensington Markets became the two essential trips for young people in London and, while Kensington Market was swallowed up by change, Camden remains a crucial stop-off. The international reputation of Camden Market dates from the mid-1980s, when Northside hired a PR firm to promote the market to visitors in the US and beyond.

Remarkable people could be found hidden in the arches, from rising stars to Camden institutions. The ultimate 1980s fashion label BodyMap started with a stall at the Lock selling ra-ra skirts. The exemplar of weirdness was perhaps Tony Bassett, who ran a unique business called No. 1 Electronics, selling not only theremins but also 'working' time machines. His wide-ranging experiments also covered the Canceltron for 'reversing diseases in plants, animals and humans', and the Bio Activity Translator which produced electronic sounds based on the mood of the plant it was attached to. He also experimented with a special hallucinogenic cheese that contained prussic acid.

The market exists in a parallel world to the rest of Camden, the only place that tourists go and the only place that locals do not. Writing in the 1980s Nina Stibbe, newly down from Leicestershire, had quickly acquired the dismissive attitude of a true Camdenite. Her diary records, 'Helen came to stay, so had to go to Camden Market'. However, Stibbe goes on to conjure up the peculiar, home-made atmosphere of Camden in the 1980s: 'A busker playing the didgeridoo drowned out a poor blind man who quietly sings "You Fill Up My Senses".'[15] In retrospect, this seems a lot closer to the rackety, pre-war London street markets than the version Camden offers today.

Folk Art on the High Street

Camden's lesser known markets are an important part of the overall picture. Buck Street Market occupies a slightly scruffy triangle of land behind the tube station, a bomb site that has never been developed. Plans to demolish the market for a new tube station hang over its long-term future, but its value to Camden is more than just the quality of the leather jackets on sale. While it lacks the picturesque buildings of the Lock Market, it does have the history. The metal-framed stalls, known as 'The Cages', are clustered around a stumpy brick tower. This is the Camden

Town deep-level shelter, one of a number built at Northern line stations between 1940 and 1942. There is another not far away at Belsize Park, and more famous examples at Goodge Street, where Eisenhower had his headquarters, and at Clapham South where arrivals on the *Empire Windrush* were first housed. The Camden shelter was one of five that were opened to the public when rocket attacks began in 1944, and could shelter 8,000 people. The tower entrance leads to two deep tunnels, which run along the High Street. They have been used for archive storage and also for filming, appearing in television sci-fi series *Blake's 7*, and playing the tunnels of the 'Undercity' on Pluto in a 1977 *Doctor Who* episode, 'The Sun Makers'.

Buck Street Market opened in the early 1980s, as Camden's fashion reputation grew. Wayne and Geraldine Hemingway, later of *Red or Dead* fame, started out re-selling clothes from the second-hand markets of West Yorkshire to Marc Almond and Jean-Paul Gaultier. The market specialised in mod gear, especially boots – 'Industrial, army, fifties, sixties, seventies – even forties, thirties and twenties', trench coats and jackets, while the Electric Ballroom next door had stalls for a different crowd selling 'trinkets, badges and dark-looking clothes' to 'rockers, punks and weirds'.[16]

Camden High Street (from the tube station to the Lock) and Chalk Farm Road are not a designated market, but the shops contribute a great deal to the atmosphere. When the Lock Market took off in the 1970s and 1980s, the High Street was half-empty and there were cheap leases on offer. Clothes and food shops, looking like market stalls, moved in and a new form of shop art took hold. Nowadays, Camden is London's main location for bespoke shop signs. These can take the form of giant Doc Martens or Converse trainers, a chain-festooned cyber-rocker platform boot, a dragon, a scorpion, an enormous wooden armchair, or an outsize set of body piercing rings. Evil from the Needle tattoo parlour has four aces, dice, a star and a set of roses, all in super-sized relief. Vinyl Experience, on Buck Street during the mid-1990s, famously had a motorbike permanently smashed through its front window. Camden's shop art, underappreciated and overlooked, is the latest manifestation of a trend that goes back to the shopfronts of medieval London which would use enormous symbols – including large wooden shoes – to make their function clear to those who could not read. Camden's folk art is one of the reasons the High Street feels different to anywhere else in London.

Camden's Markets Today

Complaints about a tourist takeover of the market date from the late 1980s, when rates for stalls increased and long-serving market manager Eric Reynolds could say, 'If anyone goes to London, they will go to the Tower, they will go to the Palace, and they will go here'.[17] By the mid-90s, when Camden Town tube station was forced to become exit-only on Sundays, the numbers visiting had increased to the point where they were difficult to control, and Camden already seemed to have reached capacity at weekends. Since then the crowds have only grown.

Camden's tourist success during the 2000s was partly due to its growing reputation as an open drug market. While this was never entirely true, 'skunk weed' was routinely offered to anyone crossing the Lock bridge from the early 2000s. As King's Cross was rebuilt, dealers and prostitutes were said to have moved on to Camden, and there was a large, highly public police raid on the bridge in 2002, with helicopters and boats. The Lock moved from cannabis to crack, but the market placed private security on the towpath which cut back the dealing. Nevertheless, 2016 saw the Metropolitan Police declaring their intention, once again, to make Camden Town 'a drug-free zone' and confiscating bongs from stalls in Buck Street Market.

It has become common wisdom that Camden Market is not what it was. Some complaints relate to the disappearance of the hippy strangeness that made the Lock and Stable Markets special, and there is no doubt that both have become more commercially orientated. Chain retailers have popped up at the edges of the market, which is dispiriting in a place with a reputation built on being different. The lock keeper's cottage has become a Starbucks, and the Ice Wharf has a Wetherspoon's. Although this trend has not yet overwhelmed the character of the Lock, further tests are to come. The Hawley Wharf development on the site of the 2008 fire seems, at the very least, to be tidying Camden up in a way that removes any potential for the unexpected. The Lock Market is now owned by Teddy Sagi, a gambling software billionaire, who became involved in 2014. He has plans for major work, creating new entrances to the site and adding new buildings including a glass box over Dead Dog Basin.

Complaints also relate to the crowds, which are fairly overwhelming on Saturday and Sunday afternoons. Londoners tend to avoid Camden Market by default, as they do Oxford Street. However, there is also an element of generational bias thinly concealed within attitudes towards Camden. There is no doubt that Camden is popular – very popular indeed – and that most people coming to the market are in their teens and twenties. Camden is still the place they choose to go, and the Lock, the old stable blocks and vaults, and the former bonded warehouses are where they spend their time.

Navvies working on the Midland Railway, between Kentish Town Road and Hammond Street, in 1865.

Chapter 3 **From Immigration to Desperation, from Gang War to Revolution**

Camden Town is known for the music, the markets and the weekend crowds, but some of the poorest places in London are only a street away. From the early nineteenth century, hard, dangerous work building the new industrial city was widely available. The Regent's Canal and then the railways drew people to Camden from across the British Isles, in particular from Ireland. Poor conditions for the new arrivals changed much of Camden from a middle-class suburb into streets of large houses divided into small, cheap lodgings.

Immigration continued to shape Camden Town over the next century and a half, as an ideal landing place for those arriving in the city to seek a fortune, or at least a living. Immigrants moulded Camden into a place for outsiders, and radicals from Karl Marx to the anti-apartheid movement all found homes in Camden's terraces. Today Camden retains the cultural diversity bred from the upheavals of its creation. It also retains the poverty, with parts of Camden home to generations of rough sleepers.

The Mickey

Arlington House, a dark red-brick cliff of a building on Arlington Street, symbolises these hidden lives through its long associations with immigration, transience and gaining a foothold in London. It looms

'Arlington House, Camden Town', James Cornes, *Modern Housing in Town and Country*, 1905. Cornes's survey includes the following information with the photograph: 'Cost per cube foot, 11d. Charge for accommodation, 6d per night per person.'

over the north end of its street, a block away from the High Street and the market traffic. It represents the Camden that does not offer itself up to visitors. The building opened in 1905 as the final Rowton House, a series of enormous London hostels known as 'the poor man's hotels', built by the philanthropist Lord Rowton and inspired by the pioneering Guinness Trust social housing. Other Rowton Houses had already opened in King's Cross, Elephant and Castle, Hammersmith, Vauxhall and Whitechapel (where Stalin stayed in 1907). Arlington House was said to be the largest hostel in Europe, with cubicles for more than 1,000 men. Women were not admitted. It was not a homeless hostel, but was designed to provide decent, affordable lodging for those with nowhere else to stay, at 6d per night.

Lord Rowton (Montagu Lowry-Corry) had been private secretary to Disraeli, and his political careers including promoting reforms designed to limit working hours and regulate lodging houses. He used his own funds to build an alternative to the workhouse 'casual' wards, where accommodation was offered only in exchange for work such as oakum picking (unpicking tarred lengths of rope for reuse). His mission was to improve the standard of accommodation available to working men, who had to choose between the streets, the workhouse and the common lodging-houses.

George Orwell, in his 1933 investigation of poverty, *Down and Out in Paris and London*, explained the gradations of accommodation that were available in London in the 1930s. The first step above sleeping rough was the 'Twopenny Hangover' – benches on which men could, for 2d, sleep in rows, sitting down and leaning on a rope. At 5am 'a man, humorously called the valet, cuts the rope'. A slightly more expensive option was 'The Coffin', which was simply a wooden box covered in a tarpaulin: 'It is cold, and the worst thing about it are the bugs, which, being enclosed in a box, you cannot escape.'[1] Then there were the common lodging-houses of which the best, according to Orwell and his informants, were the Rowton Houses, which had 'excellent bathrooms'. Delegations from Europe and the US

Sleeping cubicle at Rowton House, photographed in 1926.

came to study the Rowton model, and men would walk across London for a room. Drawbacks included the rules that banned cooking and social activities such as playing cards. Because the accommodation was in the form of cubicles, men had to keep their belongings under their beds to avoid the fishing rods that might reach over the partition from next door. Nevertheless they were, Orwell claimed, 'always full to overflowing'.[2] However, Orwell rated the Rowton Houses below the more expensive common lodging-houses which, although 'squalid dens', made it possible to have a social life.

The Camden Rowton House was known as 'The Big House' or 'The Mickey (Mouse)'. According to the poet Patrick Kavanagh, who lived there during the 1930s, it was a hub for 'artists of the demi-monde . . . every pickpocket, chancer and beggar from the four winds of crime'.[3] However, it was also home to eccentrics whom he described as 'quaintly individual', such as a well-dressed man in spats called Mr Boot, who ran a team of street hawkers selling quack remedies but lived on 2d bowls of soup from the Rowton canteen. Little had changed by the 1970s, when David Thomson came to know a man he referred to as 'Justice Shallow', who was from Norfolk, in his eighties, living in the Rowton House with 'coat hanger shoulders and long skinny neck'.[4] By this time Arlington House, although principally used by Irish men, was a refuge for immigrants from around the world. A Ceylonese cook, who spoke six European languages but was out of work, describes the English bitterly to Kavanagh as 'rough, rough, rough, cruel people'.[5]

Arlington House has an established place in Camden's cultural geography. Camden's own Madness began their song 'One Better Day' with the lines 'Arlington House, address: no fixed abode / An old man in a three-piece suit sits in the road'.[6] They connect both the doss house and Camden as a whole with 'The feeling of arriving when you've nothing left to lose'. The Pogues, meanwhile, sang about VP sherry and violence in the grim 1984 track 'Transmetropolitan', which ends with an escape to Scotland 'from Arlington House with a 2 bob bit'.[7] Gallon Drunk's song, 'Arlington

Street', finds a character from 'Temperance House' in the gutter 'face down and spent'.[8] And in the last lines he wrote before his fatal heroin overdose, Daniel Lux described how 'Arlington's doss house lights twinkling' in the distance told him he was home.[9]

The Workhouse and the Street

Poverty persists in Camden, with little to cushion the divide between high-price housing and council-run estates. Camden Town and tramps go together. Peter Ackroyd writes about the 'vagrant drinkers' of Camden Town, claiming in characteristically airy fashion that 'its inhabitants, however individually transitory, have congregated in the High Street since the day it first opened'.[10] There is, however, a history of dereliction in the streets of Camden which can be traced back to the eighteenth century, a time that predates the building of Camden. The original site of the Mother Black Cap pub, where Camden Town tube station now stands, was leased by the Parish of Old St Pancras in 1788 to build a new poor house, which became the St Pancras Workhouse. The far edge of the neighbourhood was the chosen spot for relocating the most unfortunate. The new building was at the fringes of the parish, but at the centre of what was to be Camden Town.

By the early nineteenth century the workhouse was severely over-crowded, with inmates sleeping five or six to a bed, and the beds described optimistically as 'fit for use if they be cleaned from vermin'. The workhouse records show purchases of 'Druggs to Kill Buggs'. The dismal conditions were revealed in *A Memoir of Robert Blincoe*, the 1832 autobiography of a cotton miller and child-labour campaigner. As an orphan he lived in the St Pancras Workhouse during the 1790s. While there he was sent out, aged six, to work as a chimney sweep. He left a year later when his indenture was sold to a cotton mill near Nottingham, where he was employed alongside other small children as a 'mule scavenger', crawling under the looms to collect cotton waste and losing part of a finger in the process. His account of his childhood, published in 1828, influenced a government investigation into conditions in the mills. It has been claimed that Blincoe's life influenced Charles Dickens's depiction of workhouse life in *Oliver Twist* and, while there is no evidence of a direct connection, his experiences certainly represented those that Dickens was anxious to expose, taking place on his Camden doorstep.

The workhouse was finally relocated to a new site on St Pancras Way in 1809. Its buildings, which remain forbidding, are now St Pancras Hospital. However, nearly two centuries after its closure something still seems to draw lost people to the site of the first workhouse, at Camden Town tube. George Gissing, writing in the 1890s, has one of his characters meet 'a shabbily dressed man of middle age, whose face did not correspond with his attire' at the station, who asks for bread and a cup of tea and complains about the 'very hard times'.[11] Many decades later Nick Kimberley, arriving for the first time in Camden in 1970 to work at Compendium Books, recalled that the tube station was the first place in London where he saw anyone begging. In the cold winter of 1983 David Thomson wrote that he had 'never seen so many destitute people sitting for warmth in Camden Town tube station'.[12] Ticket barriers now keep people out of the station itself, relegating them to surrounding pavements and doorways.

Another central Camden site haunted by those on the edge is the courtyard of the Job Centre on Camden High Street. It was built on the site of the lost Bedford Theatre and the Bedford Arms pub at its rear. The demolition of the music hall in the 1960s (discussed in Chapters 1 and 5) left a strange absence at the heart of Camden. The Job Centre, with its archway entrance echoing the missing form of the Bedford, draws small desolate crowds of the unemployed, waiting for something that never seems likely to arrive. In the 1890s the labour exchange was on Royal College Street, where the scene was similar: 'About 30 men reading the newspapers on the hoarding, or standing on the kerb'.[13] The ghost of the Bedford casts a gloomy shadow over the southern end of Camden. The High Street between Camden Town and Mornington Crescent tube stations is the darker end of Camden, where the market crowds melt away and the poverty becomes visible and unmistakable.

A famous Second World War story casts an accidental light on the life of one Camden drifter. In 1943 Camden funeral directors Leverton's supplied the government with the body of Welsh tramp Glyndwr Michael, who became 'The Man Who Never Was'. Michael, homeless and desperate, had died in St Pancras Hospital after eating rat poison in unknown circumstances. His corpse was dressed in Royal Marines uniform and released in the sea to wash up on the Spanish coast, with false details of Allied invasion plans for Sicily in his pocket. The Nazis were taken in by the deception.

The enduring symbol of Camden dereliction is Alan Bennett's 'Lady in the Van', Miss Shepherd, who occupied his Gloucester Crescent drive for twenty years. She was deeply eccentric and very difficult to deal with, living and sleeping in an ancient Bedford van that no longer functioned. She spent her days on Camden High Street, selling home-produced religious tracts which she refused to admit to writing. Her air of refinement, at bizarre odds with her life on the streets, turned out to be authentic. She had been a concert pianist who lost her mental bearings, had tried to become a nun and been committed to an asylum. She could be paranoid and aggressive, but her presence in the heart of gentrified Camden, on the doorstep of the man who was himself the vanguard of social change, cast her as its spirit of place.

Miss Shepherd was not always as unbalanced as she seemed. She once told Bennett that she had seen a boa constrictor on Parkway. Although prone to delusions and frequently demanding that Bennett call the police, she may on this occasion have been right. Palmer's Regent Pet Stores on Parkway was founded in 1918 by George Palmer. During the 1960s the family claimed that they let their boa constrictors loose in the shop at night, as security, although this was thought to be canny publicity. On the day in question in 1971, the shop had apparently been burgled. The shop was famous in its day, selling a ginger kitten to Churchill when he was Prime Minister during the 1950s, and Abyssinian kittens to Charlie Chaplin, cats to Peter Cook and Dudley Moore and newts to Ken Livingstone. The shop moved over the road in 2005 and closed in 2015, but its original decorative black and white frontage remains, complete with lettering advertising 'Monkeys', 'Talking Parrots' and, curiously, 'Naturalists'.

Neil Ansell arrived in Camden in 1980 to volunteer for a radical charity called the Simon Community, helping the homeless while living among them in voluntary poverty. He began visiting Sunset Strip. This was the name given locally to a row of derelict terraced houses beside the Regent's Canal on the southern edge of Camden, which were squatted despite having no water, electricity or lockable doors. They were the squats of last resort, inhabited by people who were in and out of the drunk tank and the TB ward at the Hospital for Tropical Diseases, including Irish John, Scots Mary and Gypsy Davy, the latter two being Scottish gypsy travellers who begged outside the tube station for thirty years. Ansell found Camden 'predominantly Irish' while King's Cross was the 'Scottish heartland'.[14] He also found the life draining, as the people he helped died around him. Sunset Strip burned down and, in 1984, Ansell walked out of Camden to the foot of the M1, before hitching all the way to the Isle of Jura. The Simon Community, however, continues to operate, from two houses in Kentish Town.

The Four Pubs

Sometimes everything in Camden seems to come down to pubs. Camden's leading pub legend draws on its origins as a railway boom town. When the railway navvies arrived in the mid-nineteenth century from across the country, there were tensions both with existing residents and among the new arrivals. Their presence is memorialised in the often-repeated claim that separate Camden pubs were set up to keep the Irish, Scottish, Welsh and English workers apart, named accordingly – the Dublin Castle on Parkway, the Edinboro Castle on Mornington Terrace, the Pembroke Castle on Gloucester Avenue, and the now closed Windsor Castle (also called the Warwick Castle, now a branch of Côte) on Parkway.

Sometimes the Caernarvon Castle pub on Chalk Farm Road, demolished after the 2008 Camden fire, is substituted as the Welsh pub. The story sounds good, but any level of examination reveals it to be unlikely. The pubs were built decades apart, some of their names can be traced to sources unrelated to nationality, and the idea of an 'English' pub makes little sense. However, the pubs themselves play important roles in Camden culture, and the popularity of the story reveals a continuing fascination with Camden's navvy roots.

The Dublin Castle was actually an Irish pub, although by the 1970s it was equally frequented by English and Greek Cypriot drinkers. It was an important Irish music venue in the post-war period before becoming, under the ownership of Alo Conlon (who was himself from Dublin), perhaps Camden's best alternative music venue. The Edinboro Castle was known as a betting pub, in the days when betting was illegal outside racecourses, and was undoubtedly known to the Race Track gangs discussed below. It took three years to rebuild after it was burned out in 1984 in a fire started by a disgruntled customer. During the nineteenth century the landlord was Thomas Middlebrook, who used the pub to display his famous, ever-growing collection of curiosities. These included a 4,000-year-old Babylonian brick, Cromwell's helmet and spurs, a tourniquet used while amputating Nelson's arm, Wellington's death mask, the bugle that sounded the Charge of the Light Brigade and three eggs from the extinct Great Auk.

Irish Camden

At the centre of a band of North London Irish neighbourhoods stretching from Cricklewood to Islington, Camden had a large Irish population from the very beginning. While Camden was under construction, men from Ireland were arriving to build it. Areas of London were already associated with the Irish before the Industrial Revolution, particularly St Giles, off Tottenham Court Road, Saffron Hill and parts of Whitechapel. The end of the Napoleonic Wars in 1815 was followed by an agricultural depression that drove many Irish families to seek a living overseas. The availability of work from the 1780s on the new canal network, and then on the roads and railways, as well as the many building projects in the expanding city, drew many to London. Emigration increased greatly with the Great Famine of the 1840s, and by 1851 over 100,000 Irish people were living in London, often in slum conditions. They received little sympathy, even from more enlightened sources. They were often seen as the cause rather than the victims of their living conditions. In *Oliver Twist* Charles Dickens describes the pubs of Saffron Hill where 'the lowest orders of Irish were wrangling with might and main', and yards where 'drunken men and women were positively wallowing in filth'.[15]

Navvies were rarely welcomed with open arms, due in part to their reputation as hard-drinking men who liked a fight. They were at the bottom of the heap, doing dangerous and exhausting jobs, and of little account as individuals. Irish inhabitants of the infamous inner London rookeries were seen as less than human by many mid-Victorian commentators. There was also, of course, an added history of religious conflict with Catholic Ireland, and previous centuries had seen plots against the Crown and Parliament, both actual and fabricated (including the Titus Oates affair involving the Primrose Hill murder of Sir Edmund Berry Godfrey, described in Chapter 1). The 1840s saw sporadic outbreaks of violence in various parts of the country between locals and Irish workers, including in Camden.

In August 1846 a minor argument outside the Roundhouse, between Irish navvies working on the railway line and English labourers working at the Camden Goods Station site, escalated into a mass brawl. The two groups fought with the tools that came to hand – shovels and picks – with the police unable to control the situation. The fighting spread across the railway lands and

Arlington Road, Camden Town, early 1960s. This snapshot of Camden life juxtaposes the Belgian Our Lady of Hal church with the Irish Record Centre.

lasted for three hours. While no one was killed, a number were seriously injured. Twenty Irish men were arrested, and given prison sentences after an Old Bailey trial. They claimed that the English labourers had abused and provoked them, but no English worker was brought to account.

David Thomson, writing about the Camden navvies, described them as 'reckless in their leisure. They came and went to the next job in hordes, shared hardships and pleasures peculiar to their homeless life, helped each other in adversity, had a strong sense of justice, were loyal to the gang and to fair employers, and fiercely violent against those who cheated them of food or pay.'[16]

The descendants of the navvies continued to come to Camden until the end of the 1970s to work in construction jobs, lodging at the Mickey and patronising Camden's many Irish pubs. Patrick Kavanagh's autobiographical novel, *The Green Fool*, follows a young man who walks from Louth, near the border with Northern Ireland, to Dublin, and from there makes his way to Arlington House where he has been advised to stay. Kavanagh wrote that 'Many Irish boys made Rowton House, Camden Town, first stop from Mayo. The soft voices of Mayo and Galway sounding in that gaunt, impersonal place fell like warm rain on the arid patches of my imagination'.[17]

Playwright Brendan Behan and his songwriter brother Dominic lived in Arlington House in the 1940s. Twenty years later the latter wrote 'McAlpine's Fusiliers' about the Camden Irish army working on construction sites for firms such as Laing, Wimpey and McAlpine. It pithily sums up the life: 'Twas in the pub they drank the sub / And out in the spike you'll find them' (the 'spike' being the doss house). Behan does not recommend the life, recounting the racist abuse, friends killed on site, and the never-ending work in the dark and the rain. 'McAlpine's god is a well-filled hod' he sings, concluding 'If you pride your life don't join, by Christ! / With McAlpine's fusiliers'.[18]

The Irish Sound

In the 1930s bars and clubs began to open in Camden catering specifically to the growing Irish population. The Buffalo Bar was run by 'Ginger' Maloney and gained a reputation for trouble, eventually causing the police to close it down. The venue was rescued in 1937 by Bill Fuller, a construction worker from Kerry who was also an amateur boxer and wrestler, and was to become a doyen of the international music scene. Fuller, who was only twenty at the time, persuaded the police to let him reopen the club as the Carousel, on the basis that he would deal with any trouble himself. If he ever had to call the police, the venue would close. It was no easy task, and Fuller recalled: 'We'd get all the Connemara lads in, and they were all well used to fighting, those were wild days you know.'[19] Nevertheless, the Carousel survived and, as the Electric Ballroom, remains open today.

However, the heyday of Irish culture in Camden was the 1950s, when the generation who had moved to London for the post-war rebuilding boom set up their own venues and took over Camden's best-known pubs. The London Irish Centre was set up in 1955 by two Catholic priests, as a hostel and social centre for Irish immigrants, in the Camden Square premises that it still occupies today. It was popular with working-class locals, occupying the other end of the social scale to establishments such as the Irish Club in Eaton Square, which was frequented by cultural figures such as Cyril Cusack. The London Irish Centre ran ceilidhs and 'county bacon and cabbage dinners', and later became known as a music venue. Camden is said to have been the first place where Irish traditional music was played in London after the war. Men were commonly not allowed back to their lodgings until late in the evening, and naturally congregated in the pubs. Camden venues – the Dublin Castle, the Camden Stores on Parkway, the Mother Red Cap and, above all, the Bedford Arms on Arlington Street – quickly became famous on both sides of the Irish Sea.

Mike Smythe performing at a Sunday lunchtime session in the Bedford Arms, Camden Town, in the 1960s.

Margaret Barry and Michael Gorman performing at Cecil Sharp House in 1965.

Legendary figures could be found playing on stage and on the streets of Camden, including Donegal tin-whistle player Packie Byrne and the 'Queen of the Gypsies', Margaret Barry, a traveller singer from Cork. Barry moved to London in the early 1950s and worked with Michael Gorman, a famed fiddler from Sligo, and the two were often to be heard playing in The Bedford Arms. She had been brought up by street musician parents, and was a powerful vocalist who sang without amplification, accompanying herself on the banjo. She attracted the admiration of American folk music collector Alan Lomax, who employed her as his housekeeper. Lomax lived in Camden during the 1950s in self-imposed exile from McCarthyism, and was a key part of the Camden-centred folk-revival scene. Margaret Barry returned to Ireland in the 1960s, living in Dublin where she was reputed to have drunk Brendan Behan under the table.

Much of the music of the time was recorded by Topic Records engineer Bill Leader. He would hold recording sessions in his flat at No. 5 North Villas, off Camden Square, with musicians he encountered in nearby pubs, including Margaret Barry and Michael Gorman, and Dominic Behan, a dominant figure on the Camden scene. Leader also recorded the new generation of musicians on the brink of wider fame, including Davey Graham, Peggy Seeger and the Watersons. Folk guitar prodigy Bert Jansch recorded his first album in Leader's home studio in 1965, including the totemic instrumental 'Blackwaterside' which influenced successive generations of musicians, from Simon and Garfunkel to Led Zeppelin and beyond. The studio set-up was Leader's kitchen, 'soundproofed with blankets and egg boxes'.[20] 'Blackwaterside' was, inevitably, a traditional Irish song repurposed by Jansch.

The influence of the Irish scene went beyond Camden's own. Bob Dylan visited London in 1962, playing for the first time in Britain in the Pindar of Wakefield pub on the King's Cross Road, and meeting British folk musicians including Camden-based Geordie singer Bob Davenport, who later played on the

Freewheelin' Bob Dylan album. Davenport, a pillar of the Camden folk scene, wrote 'Wild Wild Whiskey' about the lure of the place and the dangers of becoming drawn in because 'whiskey laughs the longest in the pubs of Camden Town'.[21]

By the 1970s music had moved on, and any venues that once hosted traditional Irish music had gone punk. The Pogues made their name combining both styles, playing at the Dublin Castle, the Devonshire Arms on Hawley Crescent and at Dingwall's. Shane MacGowan had reinvented himself as a lairy working-class Camden drinker, having started off as a public school boy. The Pogues's 1985 song 'London Girl' includes the lines 'The devil moon took me out of Soho / Up to Camden where the cold north winds blow'.[22] Camden lured its own people back again and again, but it could be unforgiving to those who heard the call.

Suggs's 1995 song 'Camden Town' includes 'a string of Irish pubs far as you can see'.[23] Twenty years on, this is no longer the case. Camden's remaining Irish pubs and clubs are tucked away in side streets or at the fringes of Camden Town – Quinn's on Kentish Town Road, the Sheephaven Bay on Mornington Street, or the London Irish Centre at Camden Square. Pubs in more commercially viable locations have been refurbished to suit a different clientele, with more money to spend. The annual Return to Camden Town Festival, set up in 1998, programmes traditional Irish music in pubs and clubs across Camden and North London in general. Its title sums up the cultural role of Camden as a home-from-home for Irish culture in England, while its struggle to remain in business illustrates the fading Irish cultural dominance after 150 years, at least in traditional form.

Greek, Jewish, Belgian and German Camdens

The All Saints Greek Orthodox Cathedral Church on the corner of Pratt Street and Camden Street is the symbolic centre of Camden's Greek Cypriot life. Opening in 1824 as Camden's parish church it was, appropriately, designed in Greek revival style by William Inwood and his son Henry (also responsible for St Pancras New Church on Euston Road). In 1948 it was taken over by Camden's newly expanded population of Greek Cypriots, who had come to London in large numbers, escaping post-war poverty in what was still a British colony. Greek Cypriots congregated in Camden, while Turkish Cypriots chose Harringay and Stoke Newington. Tensions in Cyprus, where EOKA guerrillas were fighting for independence from Britain and unification with Greece, spilled over to London. In 1956 the British government ordered the arrest of the clergyman in charge of the cathedral, Father Kallinikos Macheriotis. He was deported to Athens on a 2am flight. Macheriotis was the unofficial leader of London's Greek Cypriots, and Archimandrite (priest in charge) at the cathedral. He was accused of fundraising for EOKA and of spreading anti-British propaganda. After Cyprus became independent in 1960 its leader, Archbishop Makarios, visited London several times to preach at All Saints, and a memorial service there for him in 1977 attracted 6,000 mourners.

Camden also has its own Greek Cypriot theatre, Teatro Technis, based in the Old St Pancras Church mission house on Crowndale Road (with a statue of the saint, a teenage Roman martyr, over the door). It was founded in 1957 by George Eugeniou, who had moved to London from Limassol and spent time at Joan Littlewood's highly influential Theatre Workshop. Performances were originally in Greek, but then broadened to attract a wider audience to deliver Eugeniou's aim of tackling racial and social injustice by developing 'a radical and total theatre to break barriers between nationalities, religions, genders, sexual orientations, classes, ages and languages'.[24] The theatre moved to its current home in 1978, having spent years in a garage on Camden Mews which it shared with the owner's car, and in a disused railway shed at the former Maiden Lane cattle depot behind King's Cross. Performances also took place in a Kentish Town pub, an Eversholt Street basement and a café on York Way. The theatre, which is still pursuing its mission, also manages flats on the Farrier Street estate next door as the Cypriot Housing Project.

The Jewish connection with Camden Town is less direct. Camden now houses the Jewish Museum, which moved to a former piano factory on Albert Street in 1994. Founded in 1932, the museum was previously based in Bloomsbury. It merged with the London Museum of Jewish Life, formerly the Museum of the Jewish East End, which moved to the Camden site in 2007. While Camden is home to the central archive of Jewish Britain, it is located at the southern tip of Jewish North London. The proposed Camden eruv – an area marked with wire strung between poles, where religiously observant Jews are permitted basic activities otherwise denied to them on the Sabbath – begins immediately north of the Regent's Canal, stretching all the way from Chalk Farm to the northern fringes of London, but excluding Primrose Hill and central Camden Town.

The Belgian influence on Camden was briefer, but also left its mark. A huge influx of Belgian refugees arrived in Britain in 1914, fleeing the German invasion. The Belgians remain the largest group of refugees, around 250,000 in total, ever to arrive in Britain but, because most returned when the First World War ended, their presence has been largely forgotten. In Camden, though, an order of Belgian missionaries called the Scheut Fathers stayed on, founding a Belgian Catholic church on Arlington Street. Based originally in a temporary hut, the permanent New Church of Our Lady of Hal was completed in 1933 and is still there, looking much more Belgian than anything else on the street. The last Belgian priest returned home in 1995, and the church now has no particular Belgian connection apart from the replica of Our Lady of Hal at the Immaculate Heart of Mary, a venerated statue from the town of Hal in Belgium, located in a shrine inside.

A forgotten episode from the previous century brought another set of immigrants to Camden. In the 1870s and 1880s Kaiser Wilhelm I and his Chancellor, Bismarck, pursued a policy of victimisation against Roman Catholics in several states, suspecting them of disloyalty to the German Empire. This brought a substantial number of Germans to Britain, and by the 1890s they had become the second largest immigrant group after Jews. Among the arrivals were Adam and Otto Hilger, refugees from Darmstadt and optical instrument makers. The Hilger factory on the corner of St Pancras Way and Camden Road built some of the best optical and precision instruments in the world, and among other innovations developed synthetic crystals. In 1968 they moved to Margate, and the factory buildings were eventually demolished in 2015.

Radical Camden

Camden Town has links to a succession of political pioneers across nationalities, emerging from the Camden melting pot. The German connection brought the two pre-eminent radical thinkers of the modern era to Camden, where they both lived in exile. Karl Marx and his wife moved to No. 1 Maitland Park Road, north of Chalk Farm Underground Station, in 1864. Six years later Friedrich Engels moved with his family to No. 122 Regent's Park Road in Primrose Hill.

Marx and Engels had first met in Paris in 1844. Engels was the son of a wealthy Prussian textile manufacturer, who sent him to Manchester to study the industry. There he met a working-class Irishwoman called Mary Burns, with whom he had a twenty-year relationship, and whose radical ideas and experience of the dismal working conditions in Manchester's factories changed his outlook. After Mary's death, Engels married her sister Lizzie. Marx, meanwhile, was a German philosopher of Jewish ancestry whose writing and activism had led to his expulsion from France and Germany, and the removal of his citizenship after the 1848 'Year of Revolution'.

London provided a refuge for both – although, while Engels had a good income, Marx suffered in lifelong poverty. He had lived in London since 1849 at various addresses, including in Soho and at what is now No. 46 Grafton Road, in Kentish Town. With his wife Jenny von Westphalen and their three daughters, the family upgraded to No. 1 Maitland Park Road after they received an inheritance, but were forced to move back to cheaper lodgings in 1876 at No. 41 on the same street. Engels, whose idea of happiness was Château Margaux 1848 and who claimed to live by the motto 'Take It Easy', hosted regular Sunday night parties in Primrose Hill for London's socialists which lasted into Monday morning. The two lived close enough, on the northern edge of Camden Town, to visit each regularly and to picnic together on Hampstead Heath, where they liked to recite Shakespeare with Marx's daughters. They also worked together in London, and Engels edited the second and third editions of *Das Kapital* in Primrose Hill, from Marx's papers. Both died in Camden – Marx in 1883 and Engels in 1895.

During the years that Marx and Engels were working together, Frances Buss was pioneering sexual equality a few streets away. A suffragette and women's education campaigner, she founded two schools for girls in Camden. She set up the North London Collegiate School for Ladies in 1850 in a terraced house on Camden Street. When it outgrew the site and moved to Sandall Road in 1870, she set up a second school in Camden Street – Camden School for Girls. After the Second World War the later school also moved to Sandall Road. Buss, who was the first person to describe herself as a 'headmistress', intended the schools to provide education outside the home for middle-class girls, who had almost always been taught by governesses. Her initiative was a great success, helping to reshape educational and social thinking, and both schools still operate today.

Communism continued to find a home in the Camden terraces in the twentieth century. John Bernal, who lived on Arlington Street, was a crystallographer and predictor of future space habitation. He was a scientific advisor to the government during the Second World War, producing analysis that demonstrated the futility of indiscriminate bombing raids on German cities. He was also a communist with an unconventional lifestyle, which included an enthusiastically open marriage. Fellow communist Pablo Picasso stayed with Bernal at his Torrington Square flat in 1950. He had come to England for the abortive World Peace

Conference in Sheffield, and Bernal threw a party for various stranded intellectuals to make up for their wasted journeys. During dinner Picasso drew a pencil and crayon mural on Bernal's plaster wall, the only mural he ever produced in Britain, with winged male and female heads. The section of wall containing Bernal's Picasso was removed from the flat when it was demolished, given to the ICA, and eventually bought by the Wellcome Collection.

Peggy Duff, who lived on Arlington Street, was one of the founders of CND. Originally a member of the socialist Common Wealth Party, she became a Labour councillor for Camden before resigning over the Vietnam War, and was also secretary of the National Campaign for the Abolition of Capital Punishment. An apparently chaotic figure, she nevertheless organised the CND Aldermaston peace marches of the early 1960s, when anti-nuclear feeling reached its height. Her autobiography was entitled *Left, Left, Left*.

Rights, Race and Independence

Camden's progressive pedigree does not make it immune to racist attitudes, either in the not-so-distant past or, doubtless, today. In 1982 David Thomson writes about a visit to the White Hart pub where he found racist graffiti messages in the gents, including a message that declared 'No blacks at pool table if whites want to play'.[25] However, Camden also has strong links to radical campaigning for both racial and sexual equality.

Camden's nineteenth-century residents included Victorian artist Henry Courtney Selous, famed in his time for his dramatic historical tableaux, including *Boadicea Haranguing the Iceni*. His reputation rose rapidly during the mid-1800s, and his portrait of Queen Victoria was shown as the Great Exhibition, but it has declined inexorably ever since. However, Camden remembered him, naming Selous Street in his honour – but the link between Henry Selous and his nephew Frederick later led to the street being renamed. Frederick Selous was a big-game hunter in South

Africa, a larger-than-life colonial figure, friend of Cecil Rhodes, and the model for H. Rider Haggard's Allan Quatermain character. Camden's Selous Street became home to the headquarters of the Anti-Apartheid Movement, based there between 1983 and 1994 (when it was wound up after apartheid ended in South Africa). After a mid-1980s campaign led by one of its councillors, Camden Council agreed to rename Selous Street as Mandela Street, to erase indirect colonial associations.

In 2003 Nelson Mandela himself visited nearby Lyme Street, which has a blue plaque at No. 13 marking the home of Ruth First and Joe Slovo. The married couple were South African communists, anti-apartheid activists and leading members of the African National Congress. They were forced into exile in London after the South African government began detaining opponents without trial. In 1982 First was assassinated by a parcel bomb sent by the South African police to the university where she worked, in Maputo, Mozambique, where she had moved in 1978. Joe Slovo, however, lived to be Minister of Housing in Mandela's first government.

At No. 22 Cranleigh Street, in the far south of Camden where it becomes Somers Town, lived George Padmore, born in Trinidad in 1908 and a black revolutionary before his time. He joined the Communist Party in the US, was a union representative in Moscow, then edited the *Negro Worker* in Hamburg, before being deported. He denounced communism for failing to address colonial oppression, and eventually fetched up in London in 1941, living on Cranleigh Street with his partner Dorothy Pizer until 1957. Their flat, kept under surveillance by the secret services, became a meeting place for anti-colonial activists from Africa and the Caribbean. When Padmore died in 1957, the President of Ghana, Kwame Nkrumah, had the kitchen table from Cranleigh Street flown to Africa, as a memorial to the hours he had spent sitting around it with Padmore, planning the revolution.

V. K. Krishna Menon, supporter of Indian home rule and St Pancras Borough councillor, lived on Camden Terrace in the 1920s and 1930s. He was a theosophist, supporting the esoteric philosophies promoted by Annie Besant, who helped him come to Britain in 1924. He was active on the Education and Libraries Committee, promoting the principle that there should be as many libraries as there were pubs in Camden. He also led the overseas campaign for Indian independence, was denounced by Eisenhower and monitored by MI5. He returned to India at independence in 1946 and became India's first High Commissioner, its first Ambassador to the UN, and finally Defence Minister. He resigned in 1962, taking the blame for India's failing in the Sino-Indian War. He also found time to work as one of the founding editors at Penguin Books, and to practise as a barrister.

Gangs of Camden

Before the First World War, gang-related crime was rife in London and the Camden Town gang, originally known as the Broad Mob, was responsible for much of it. Yet the gang wars that beset inner London at the turn of the nineteenth century have been largely forgotten, dropping out of official histories and missing from popular conceptions of what life in Victorian and early twentieth-century London was like. During the 1890s the southern edge of Camden saw local street clashes between the Somers Town Boys, whose areas bordered Camden Town, and the Clerkenwell Boys further east. These gangs were often equipped with firearms, which were readily available from pawnbrokers, and large groups of young men would assemble to attack each other in public. A typical incident took place outside Sadler's Wells Theatre in 1907, where a fight between Camden and Somers Town groups led to two of the Somers Town gang being stabbed.

The activities of the Camden Town gang at the time focused on racecourse and betting crime, including blackmailing and cheating bookmakers. In 1891 three men were tried for an ingenious scam which they were alleged to have attempted on a Camden Town bookie. They handed over a betting slip which included a bet, written in invisible ink, for a race that had already finished. When they went to claim, the writing had reappeared. This popular ruse only worked with careful timing – if the writing reappeared in front of the bookie's eyes, it was all over. This petty trickery was, it turned out, the precursor to serious, organised racecourse rackets.

The Race Track Wars

The Camden Town gang emerged as a serious criminal force in close association with Birmingham-based organisations. A shadowy figure called George 'Brummie' Sage was mentor to Billy Kimber, Birmingham gangster of 'Peaky Blinders' fame and leader of a gang called the Brummagem Boys. When the Birmingham gangsters expanded their interests to London, Sage took control in Camden with two close, violent lieutenants called Freddie Gilbert and John Phillips. Despite his prominent role in the events that followed, Sage remains a shadowy figure. Only a single photograph of him is thought to exist. He is posing with a charabanc full of London's most dangerous characters, several of whom he would later try to kill. He wears a bowler hat, bow-tie and three-piece suit, and, although the oldest man in the picture, is balanced on the balls of his feet, arms hanging loose by his sides, casual, truculent and poised for physical action.

Soon after the end of the First World War, the Birmingham and Camden gangs formed a new alliance with the Elephant and Castle gang, which would go on to dominate the South London underworld until the 1950s. The combined organisation controlled much of London. However, it quickly became drawn into a vicious public feud with a rival gang alliance. Jewish gangs based in the East End came together with the Hoxton Titanic gang and the Italian Clerkenwell Sabini brothers. The latter, who were called Darby and Joe, feature with George Sage in the charabanc photograph – moustachioed, straw-hatted, and

George 'Brummie' Sage (3rd from right), Billy Kimber (7th from right) and company assembled at Hammersmith Broadway, c.1919.

dangerous looking. Feuding escalated rapidly into a full-scale gang war, which revolved around Camden Town.

When Kimber arrived in London in 1920 he set up a protection racket operating on racecourses in and around the capital. Racing had been suspended during the First World War, and when it returned it brought a crime boom. Course bookmakers who refused to pay for their pitch were threatened with razors. They were charged in every possible way, paying for overpriced printed racecards and for 'chalk and sponge services' to write up prices on their boards, all gang-supplied. Food stalls were 'taxed', and contributions solicited to 'pension funds'. There was straightforward robbery too. In a scenario straight from a John Buchan novel, Frank Simmonds, a music hall contortionist and sleight-of-hand master, worked for the Camden Town gang lifting wallets at race meetings. Racing had long been associated with gang intimidation and riots, especially at high profile venues such as Ascot and Epsom, but the situation soon became much worse.

The bookies, many Jewish, turned to rival Jewish gangs for protection. There was no shortage of options, and an alliance came together involving Eddie Emmanuel, originally from the Jacob's Island rookery in Bermondsey, Alf Solomon from the East End, and Alf White, who led the King's Cross gang. They teamed up with the Sabini brothers, who ran their operations from the Griffin pub on Clerkenwell Road (still open, as seedy now as it was then). A full-scale war was soon underway between the 'Race Track Gangs', leading to a long series of violent, public clashes. Joe Sabini was shot in the jaw by Kimber's men at a trotting track in Greenford in March 1921. During the same week there were razor fights on the platforms at London Bridge Station, as rival gangs fought while waiting for the train to Plumpton races. A meeting in a King's Cross flat was brokered by bookies to calm the situation, but achieved the opposite. Alf Solomon shot Billy Kimber in the side after a drunken argument broke out. Kimber survived, and the violence escalated throughout 1921 and 1922.

Camden's George Sage led an attack at Alexandra Palace race track on the Sabinis, in full view of the police, in which one of their men was shot. The Birmingham gang took their revenge in a Derby Day ambush, waiting at a pub in Ewell to surprise the Sabinis as they returned from Epsom. As their cars drove up Kimber and his men attacked, dragging their rivals out of their vehicles and attacking them with axes, hammers and bricks. Unfortunately they had stopped the wrong cars, and managed to hospitalise a group of gangsters from Leeds, who were supposedly on their side. Mass arrests followed.

The feuding reached Camden when a fight broke out at the Southampton Arms in Mornington Crescent. Inside, the Camden Town gang were hosting a party for Billy Kimber. They were attacked by a contingent of Sabinis, but the police arrived when they heard the gunshots. They arrested Darby Sabini, who was trying to flee in a taxi with a loaded revolver. Violent public incidents continued in and around London, with the police unable to control the situation. There were major fights in Aldgate, in Brixton, at Paddington Station, on Tottenham Court Road and on Walworth Road. George Sage and Freddie Gilbert led the Camden Town gang in several brazen raids, including a raid on a pub in Clerkenwell to avenge an attack on John Phillips, who had been slashed across the face with a razor at Brighton races. It ended in a chase through Holborn, gangsters firing shots at the pursuing police, and a bullet hitting a tram on Gray's Inn Road and narrowly missing a passenger.

In August 1922, the Sabinis arrived at the Southampton Arms just as the Camden men were returning from the races. Twelve men pulled up in three taxis and emerged firing, shouting 'Take that!' and 'Here's another!' They missed everyone, but in the fight that followed Joe Sabini stabbed Gilbert with a stiletto blade, conveniently attached to his revolver. Sage and Gilbert, aided by a wooden-legged colleague, then chased a Sabini man on to a tram where they fought all the way to King's Cross, wounding an 18-year-old girl called Amy Kent in the process.

Remarkably, despite lethal weapons and unrestrained violence on all sides, no one seems to have actually been killed. Eventually, the violence caught up with the main protagonists, a number of whom were imprisoned. The Race Track Wars eventually came to an end in the mid-1920s after key figures were arrested or left the country. However, outbreaks of racecourse violence continued until the Second World War, culminating in a mass gang fight with iron bars and knuckledusters at Lewes Races in 1936.

Camden's Underworld King

After the war, the cast and the crimes had changed. The Jockey Club and the police put guards at racecourses and finally put an end to the racing rackets. A new generation of criminals was more interested in the potential of vice and of large-scale robbery. The epitome of the post-war London gangster was Camden's own Billy Hill, who was brought up at No. 23 Netley Street in what is now the Regent's Park Estate, from where he rose to become the self-described 'Boss of Britain's Underworld'. He came from a criminal family. His father was a warehouse burglar and member of the Elephant and Castle gang, while his mother received stolen goods. His sister belonged to an all-female Elephant and Castle shoplifting gang known as 'The Forty Thieves', whose methods involved walking into shops in a threatening mob and taking what they wanted, including wheeling out entire racks of clothes.

By the outbreak of the Second World War, Billy Hill had graduated from burglary, via smash-and-grab raids on jewellers, to the black market and protection rackets. After the war, during which he had fled to South Africa after a warehouse robbery and then returned to Britain for his only spell in prison, Hill teamed up with Jack 'Spot' Comer, the 'King of Soho', a Jewish racketeer from the East End.

Despite the influence the two wielded, Spot always found Hill alarmingly unpredictable. Hill was always ready to reach for his 'chiv' (knife), once openly stabbing a pimp called Belgian Johnny

Billy Hill, Eddie Chapman, 'NN' and George Walker in a London street, 1955.

in a Soho restaurant, who, fortunately for Hill, survived. In the early 1950s an incident behind Mornington Crescent, on Park Village East, summed up the way he liked to operate. Spot and Hill had arranged to meet a Kray associate called Tommy Smithson, with whom there had been a falling out. Before the parlay could begin, men hidden nearby emerged with razors and, led by Hill, set upon Smithson, almost severing his hand. Hill then vanished, leaving Spot to clean up the mess. He dumped the wounded Smithson over the wall beside the railway, an experience Smithson managed to survive and which earned him the nickname 'Scarface'.

Hill built a uniquely powerful criminal base, uniting the Camden Town gang with the Italian and Hoxton gangs they had fought during the Race Track Wars. Hill and Spot fell out in the early 1950s after Hill pulled off a succession of criminal coups, culminating in the 1952 Eastcastle Street robbery. In the largest robbery of its time, masked men escaped with £287,000, after using two cars to box in a post-office van on a side road off Oxford Street and coshing the driver. The van was later found abandoned in a Camden builder's yard off Augustus Street, near Hill's childhood home. Despite 1,000 officers being reportedly assigned to the investigation, no one was ever charged. Hill and Spot were both questioned but nothing could be proved.

However, Billy Hill was not a man to hide away. In 1955 he published his autobiography *Boss of Britain's Underworld*, the ghost-written prototype for every subsequent London crime stereotype, from the Krays to Guy Ritchie. The book strips away any lingering glamour from the criminal life, with its constant references to 'wops', 'dagoes' and 'poofs', its endless 'rumbles' between gangsters 'all tooled-up and ready to go', and its obsession with 'chivving' people. It also features an astonishing array of nicknames. In the space of a single sentence Hill gives us 'Franny the Spaniel, Bert Surefire and Taters Portsmouth', not to mention 'Billy the Fitter', 'Sammy Gruntman', 'Odd Legs', 'Lemon Drop Kid', 'Birdie Short', 'Old Broken Biscuits' and many more. The book also contains a chapter in which he taunts the police with apparent admissions to the Eastcastle Street robbery. Everyone thinks that only he could have done it, reports Hill, but 'it's a free country and there's no law against thinking'.[26]

Billy Hill ends his memoirs with the claim that he is considering retirement. 'Some young villain will come along to take my place',[27] he asserts. Instead, he was planning Jack Spot's downfall. In 1956, Hill and his South London allies ambushed him outside his Paddington flat, administering a humiliating beating. Two of the men involved, Frankie Fraser and Bobby Warren, were sent to prison for the attack but, despite testimony from Spot's wife that Hill had knocked him out with a shillelagh, no charges were brought. By the 1960s Billy Hill was not only in undisputed charge of central London's extortion and pimping operations, but had expanded his alliances. He became 'the trusted representative of the Bruno Family from Philadelphia',[28] whose slot machines he imported to London and installed across the city, taking a cut. He bought his second wife – Gyp, an exotic dancer – a nightclub in Tangier, and died in apparently genuine retirement in 1984.

The definitive accounts of this era have been written by Brian McDonald,[29] whose uncles led the Elephant and Castle gang and were fully involved in the knifings and shootings of the race-track era. McDonald described the stories, which became fully known only recently, as 'hidden in Sidcup for decades,'[30] guarded by the families of those involved. George Sage died from tuberculosis in 1947. Darby Sabini, whose reign ended when he was interned at the outbreak of the Second World War, lived long enough to feature in Graham Greene's *Brighton Rock*, fictionalised as gang leader 'Colleoni', and died in Hove in 1950. Billy Kimber, eventually defeated by the Sabinis, fled to America and became involved with Al Capone and the Chicago underworld. He was said to have killed a man in Phoenix, after which he disappeared from the records. His true fate was discovered recently – he returned to Britain in the 1930s, worked as a bookie at Wimbledon Greyhound Stadium, and died in a Torquay nursing home in 1942. Despite everything, Freddie Gilbert and John Phillips died natural deaths in the 1970s.

Exterior of 8 Royal College Street, Camden. Partly hidden by the foliage is a plaque commemorating the months in 1873 when the house was rented by Paul Rimbaud and Arthur Verlaine.

Chapter 4 **From Artists and Outsiders to Bohemians and Gentrification**

From its ancient origins as a refreshment stop for travellers already regretting their decision to leave London, Camden Town was to become a Victorian frontier boom town. Open for business by the 1830s on the northern edge of the smoke-shrouded city, it soon attracted outsiders as well as the respectable middle classes, people escaping social strictures and looking for space for their own ways of living. They found new, jerry-built houses which were shabby, cold and cramped, but easy on the rent. Anonymity was on offer in the largest city on earth, and the mushrooming inner suburbs were the place to find it.

A century later, the return of the bohemian heralded the return of Camden, as it dragged itself out of the post-war slump with the help of colonising middle-class arrivals. The cultural elite now inhabits the expensively restored Victorian houses of Primrose Hill and Gloucester Crescent, and Camden has become a twenty-first-century case study in social change. However, tensions between rich and poor, between crescent and tower block, remain. Camden still belongs to all the social group and tribes piled into its dense core. There is still room, just, for people looking for a space to run to.

Bohemian Camden began in Royal College Street, which is still on Camden's periphery today – a jumble of garages, substations, stay-behind pubs, 1970s estates and terraced fragments. No. 8 is in the middle of a group of houses, sporting an incongruous pediment, four storeys high including a dark semi-basement. It is next to the Royal Veterinary College. Until recently semi-derelict, wisteria now discreetly conceals a stone plaque with an inscription in gilt lettering: 'The French poets Paul Verlaine and Arthur Rimbaud lived here May–July 1873.'

Outsider Neighbourhood

Camden is marked, as the writer Cathi Unsworth put it, by 'all the cut-throats, guttersnipes, sorcerers, drinkers and dreamers who have come this way before'.[1] Top of the list are the volatile poet lovers, Rimbaud and Verlaine, whose few weeks in lodgings sealed Camden's status as a refuge of choice for cultural outsiders. For a mere three months in 1873, Arthur Rimbaud and Paul Verlaine lived on Royal College Street – scandalously together. Verlaine was only twenty-seven when, in the aftermath of the Paris Commune, he left his wife and son for the seventeen-year-old Rimbaud (who looked much younger) and was swept up in a maelstrom of condemnation.

Rimbaud was a wild child who had declared his intention of making himself, in an excitable letter to his school teacher, 'as scummy as possible' in preparation for a life as a poet and seer.[2] He vigorously pursued his path to true poetry through 'derangement of all the senses', which included, as well as copious enjoyment of absinthe and hashish, a pattern of behaviour which made him very unpopular. He would poison his friend's drinks, shit on tables, and indulge in a penchant for stabbing himself and others. He cultivated lice in his hair so, he claimed, he could flick them at priests, and boasted of losing his virginity to a dog. Accounts of his behaviour are dominated by comments such as 'Next day, he amused himself by smashing all the porcelain'.[3]

Rapidly becoming unwelcome in Paris, Rimbaud and Verlaine came to London for the first time in 1872. They lived in a now-demolished Fitzrovia house, its site helpfully marked by the BT

Photographic portrait of Arthur Rimbaud aged sixteen, taken in 1870.

Tower, and attended radical, Communard meetings. 'London is as flat as a black bug', declared Verlaine.[4] However, after a break on the Continent they returned to live on Royal College Street in May 1873. According to Rimbaud's biographer, Graham Robb, Camden was a district of 'costermongers, rag-and-bottle merchants, bird-sellers and pawnbrokers',[5] but Verlaine described it as 'A very gay quarter. You'd think you were in Brussels'.[6] Their short time in Camden was a crucial period of creativity for both writers. As well as advertising their services as French teachers and as Latin teachers (in French), the two poets wrote together. 'It is necessary to be absolutely modern', declared Rimbaud, whose unhinged perfectionism was such that he ripped up his work and started again at the slightest mistake. While living on Royal (then Great) College Street Rimbaud is believed to have written both his masterpieces, *Illuminations* and *A Season in Hell*, while Verlaine produced most of his *Romances San Paroles*. These were the works that ensured lasting fame for both.

However, their purple patch was driven by conflict. Verlaine had noted that everyone in London was permanently drunk, and this suited him well. Absinthe enthusiasts, the two lovers would drink and indulge in sado-masochistic foreplay, cutting each other with knives, before going to bed or to the pub. Their liaison was always going to be brief and spectacular, and it ended after a terrible, trivial argument. Rimbaud spotted Verlaine returning from the market carrying a herring for their supper, and mocked him from an upstairs window. Verlaine hit him across the face with the herring. He then stormed off without packing, taking a ship to Antwerp from St Katharine Docks, Rimbaud frantically waving him back from the quayside. Verlaine sent a letter threatening suicide. Rimbaud, pawning their possessions, followed him and, after an absinthe session in a Brussels hotel, an argument broke out. Rimbaud apparently threatened Verlaine with blackmail; the latter produced a pistol and shot him in the wrist.

Verlaine spent two years in prison, becoming a Catholic while inside. He later returned to Britain, as a teacher in the tiny Lincolnshire village of Stickney. Rimbaud never wrote poetry again. He did, however, come back to London in 1874 in the company of another poet, Germain Nouveau, and lived in Waterloo where he worked in a box factory. Later he joined the Dutch Colonial Army in the East Indies, deserted, worked in a quarry in Cyprus and eventually settled for conventional employment as a trader in Aden and Ethiopia. He died of cancer aged thirty-seven, and alcoholism killed Verlaine five years later. Verlaine's once disdained poetry eventually became so well-known that the first lines of 'Chanson d'Automne' were broadcast over the French airwaves on 1 June 1944, the secret launch code for the D-Day invasion of Europe.

No. 8 Royal College Street has achieved belated recognition as a site of historic, literary and gay significance. It is now owned by the Rimbaud & Verlaine Foundation which aims to turn it, in time, into a 'poetry house'. The two poets, scorching their way across London on night-time walks, brought an energy to the city that, according to Iain Sinclair, left 'heat traces' on the streets they passed along and in the rooms where they fought and wrote.[7]

Grubby Suburb

The Camden of Rimbaud and Verlaine was battered by the turmoil of the railways, and laboured beneath the smoke and dirt of the industrial city. While the earliest houses, such as those on Camden Square, had been built as the basis of a quality neighbourhood, builders soon began to recognise the reality of the place. New dwellings were aimed at a more likely clientele, those lacking in means who were happy to settle for substantially less. From the mid-nineteenth to the mid-twentieth century, Camden became increasingly defined by dirt and squalor, as successive generations inhabited these houses.

Post-railway Camden consisted of 'mean, half-formed streets of fourth-rate cottages' and their setting was no better, 'dilapidated summer houses, clay pits and carpet-beating grounds'.[8] Charles Dickens, well aware from personal experience of these very houses, had already used Camden Town as the natural setting for a 'wretched lodging' in his 1850 novel *The Pickwick Papers*.[9] In *David Copperfield*, he described lodgings off Royal College Street, near the Veterinary College, that 'looked like the early copies of a blundering boy who was learning to make houses'. Conditions were equally questionable: 'The inhabitants appeared to have a propensity to throw any little trifles they were not in want of, into the road: which not only made it rank and sloppy, but untidy too, on account of the cabbage-leaves.' The area has what Dickens describes as 'an indescribable character of faded gentility'.[10]

H. G. Wells's 1909 novel, *Tono-Bungay*, discusses 'the shabby impecuniosity of the Camden Town lodging'.[11] The novel begins in an apartment with a 'blistered front door', located behind the Cobden statue at Mornington Crescent. It is 'the dining room' floor of a house, split up and sublet. The impoverished inhabitants, middle-class but down on their luck, live in two rooms separated by a folding screen and share a basement kitchen. There is no bathroom. Wells writes: 'There are wide regions of London, miles of streets of houses, that appear to have been originally designed for prosperous middle-class homes of the early Victorian type . . . I am doubtful if many of these houses had any long use as the residences of single families.'[12]

The protagonist of Compton Mackenzie's *Sinister Street*, from 1914, makes a social journey from the poverty of Camden to Chislehurst (the original home of William Camden, accidental progenitor of Camden Town). Looking for lodgings, he reports that 'when he began to examine the Camden Road as a prospective place of residence, it became suddenly very dull and respectable'. He describes it as 'a district of Victorian terraces, where the name of each street was cut in stone upon the first house; and so fine and well-proportioned was each superscription that the houses' declension from gentility was the more evident and melancholy'.[13] The presence of the River Fleet also influenced living conditions in certain parts of Camden, particularly in the vicinity of Royal College Street. The river, now buried in storm sewer for most of its route, runs through Camden from north to south, passing along Kentish Town Road, under the Regent's Canal, and through a clear valley between Pancras Way and Royal College Street. It can be observed through the grating of a drain cover on Georgiana Street, outside the Prince Albert pub. The river became highly polluted as London grew rapidly, Camden Town being a prime case study, without first building a sewage system.

London's rivers, many of which are buried under the city's streets,[14] have long been associated with disease, including a form of malaria called the London ague, common enough in the seventeenth century to have affected monarchs, as well as other more mysterious diseases that cannot now be identified. In his book *The Lost Rivers of London*, Nicholas Barton tracks cases of chronic bronchitis during the mid-1950s along the course of the Fleet through Camden, and the river is associated with notorious inner London slums further south, where the moist environment was thoroughly unpleasant.

The dampness of the Fleet valley was evident in the 1850s, in Henry Mayhew's survey *London Labour and the London Poor*. He talked to a firm that made a 'phosphor paste' for insect infestations. They claimed that, while most of their sales were to low-lying areas of London, Camden Town was particularly infested with black beetles because of its clayey soil, which retained moisture. They added, alarmingly, that 'bakers don't use much of our paste, for they seem to think it no use to destroy the vermin – beetles and bakers shops generally go together'.[15]

Mayhew also records the experience of Camden's Jack Black, a man who called himself 'The Queen's Ratcatcher'. He happily detailed the many gruesome rat bites he had suffered: 'When a rat's bite touches the bone, it makes you faint in a minute, and it bleeds dreadful – ah, most terrible.' His worst professional experiences had all been in Camden. He was bitten twice on the leg and 'that flung me down on my bed, and there I stopped, I should think, six weeks' and later on Edwards Street, now the Regent's Park Estate, where after a bite he was 'sick near three months and close on dying'.[16] Fortunately, he found that ignoring the doctor and drinking stout (in a pub on Albany Street) left him feeling much better.

Pressure on graveyards also contributed to the many health hazards of nineteenth-century London. St Martin's Gardens on Pratt Street provided an out-of-town, spill-over burial ground for the central London parish of St Martin-in-the-Fields, on Trafalgar Square. The graveyard was laid out on farmland which, in 1802, was beyond the edge of built-up London. It was not long before Camden Town jostled around its edges. Houses were built on part of the graveyard in 1855, requiring controversial exhumations. When digging began a terrible stench was soon reported. Stones were thrown at those working on the site, and the government dispatched a minister to the site to order a halt. The exhumed bodies may eventually have been reinterred under a long barrow-esque burial mound in the centre of St Martin's Gardens, which may also contain corpses from the original St Martin-in-the-Fields graveyard, which disappeared beneath Trafalgar Square.

Great College Street was named after the Royal Veterinary College, which is still based on the site where it was first established in 1791. The college was set up beyond the limits of London to protect its students from the temptations of the city, and to provide space for the animals kept on site. Charles Dickens claimed that, as a result, the neighbouring streets were inhabited by 'gentlemen students, who bought live donkeys, and made experiments on those quadrupeds in their private apartments'.[17]

At first the college dealt only with horses, but it expanded its repertoire over the years, moving on to other four-legged quadrupeds and eventually everything else. The services it provided were popular, particularly before motor transport. In 1898 Charles Booth reported 'a sad looking collection of horses, ponies and one donkey (out patients) waiting for the free attendance that is given on one day at least in the week'.[18] By 1937, the date of the current building, its staff were responding to a wider range of enquiries

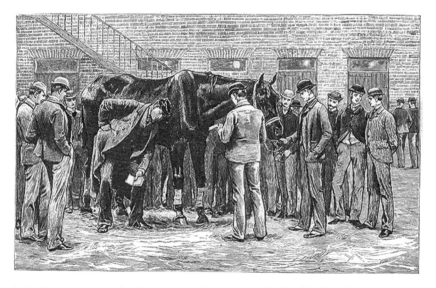

Illustration of professor and student vets examining a horse at the Royal Veterinary College. *Graphic*, 24 October 1891.

from the public, on matters such as the most humane way to destroy a tortoise (shooting, the college thought).

Sixty years later Royal College Street featured in Hitchcock's 1956 remake of his own film *The Man Who Knew Too Much*. James Stewart walks down Plender Street, the austere pediment of No. 8 Royal College Street rearing behind him, on his way to visit a taxidermist called Ambrose Chappell, seeking information about his kidnapped daughter. The taxidermist was genuine – E. Gerrard & Sons, Natural History Studios, was located in an alley close by, off College Place. Both they and the eerie Victorian buildings around them have now vanished as though they never were.

David Storey's pre-gentrification Camden Town, depicted in his 1960 novel *Flight into Camden*, is a refuge from a West Yorkshire mining town for the narrator, Margaret. However, Camden proves just as harsh an environment as the industrial north she left behind, and her impression is of 'streets narrower and buildings dirtier than I had ever expected; of row after row of sordid houses, filthier than anything I had seen at home'.[19] The area was 'one of disintegration and decay, infected with a parasitic disease that fed on the buildings, the brick and the stone'.[20]

Edge of Camden

Although Camden Town was born from upheaval, it did succeed in becoming a coherent place with a clear, although not always desirable, identity. Around its periphery, however, are failed districts, places which could not survive the railway onslaught. Land between Camden Town and Euston Station was owned by the Dukes of Bedford, who had already developed the grand, gated Bloomsbury Estate on their land south of Euston Road. However, north of Euston Road their plans foundered. By the end of the nineteenth century Werrington Street, at the southern edge of Camden, was 'the protecting line of respectability'. Beyond was Somers Town, 'a dark, if not very black, corner of London',[21] and in between were the beginnings of Bedford New Town, an ambitious project that never stood a chance.

The long railway cutting behind Euston Station, bisecting Camden on its way to Birmingham, heavily influenced the neighbourhood, both through the soot it deposited over neighbouring buildings and with the railway workers it attracted. They were obliged to lodge in Bedford Estate streets where large houses, now squeezed behind railway lines, were divided for multiple accommodation.

Bedford New Town was based around three oval 'squares' – Ampthill Square, Harrington Square and Oakley Square. The Bedford Estate fought a long and ultimately unsuccessful battle to keep the railways out. When the line was eventually built it ran straight under the middle of Ampthill Square in an open trench. Soon it had expanded, from six tracks wide in the 1870s to twelve by the 1890s, making it an impossible place to live. The doomed square suffered bomb-damage in the Second World War. Demolished in the 1960s, it was replaced by the three unmissable towers of the Ampthill Estate. Oakley Square lost its church, the centrepiece of Bedford New Town, 'a large and handsome Gothic building, with a lofty tower and spire'.[22] It was demolished in 1977.

The railway put paid to any ambitions for Bedford New Town, which slid into an existence as shabby, fragmented railway back land. The railway cutting continues to expand, with a slice of the Regent's Park Estate and of the streets next to Euston earmarked for the High Speed 2 rail route.

The fate of south Camden is symbolised by the spectacular art deco Egyptian-style Greater London House, originally the Carreras cigarette factory. Charles Dickens refers, in *Bleak House*, to 'a number of poor Spanish refugees walking about in cloaks, smoking little paper cigars in Somers Town'.[22] The aftermath of the Napoleonic Wars brought one smoking Spaniard to London in particular, José Carreras Ferrer. His family tobacco firm had been founded in Spain in 1788 but, on being forced to leave the country, he relocated it to London. After the smoking boom of the First World War, his firm,

'The Dust-Heaps, Somers Town, in 1836', in George Walter Thornbury, *Old and New London*, Cassell & Co., 1887-93.

House of Carreras, set up new, handsome premises in Camden.

The building occupies the whole of Mornington Square, one of three open spaces built into the original layout of Bedford New Town. Similar garden crescents remain nearby, at Harrington and Oakley Squares opposite, but the Mornington Crescent garden was much larger. In fact, it was the largest green space in Camden Town, and its replacement in 1927 with an outsized, outlandish factory building proved very controversial. Legislation was passed as a result to prevent such squares being built over again.

The episode did, however, leave Mornington Crescent with one of London's totemic buildings, a pre-war palace with more than a little of the occult about it. The Carreras Cigarette Company's Arcadia Works factory was, unsurprisingly, built in the aftermath of the sensation caused by the discovery of Tutankhamun's tomb, when Egyptian revival architecture enjoyed an ecstatic moment in the sun. The building is said to have been inspired by the ancient Egyptian temple of the goddess Bast, who has the head of a cat. As well as two vast black cats, seated either side of the main entrance, the faces of ten black cats with yellow eyes line up along the façade. The former chimney at the back takes the potent form of an obelisk. The building was described by the architectural critic Nikolaus Pevsner as 'abominable', but few would agree.

The building was known first as the Black Cat Factory, and later the Craven 'A' works – 'The World Famous Home of the World's Most Famous Cork-Tipped Cigarettes – Craven "A"'. An ambitious facility, it employed 3,000 workers. Advertisements boasted of 'every modern facility' and 'ideal conditions' for each employee, including four canteens (with free tea), a doctor, dentist, oculist and chiropodist, free legal advice, a holiday home in Brighton, a sports ground in Stanmore, as well as angling, bridge, darts, horticulture, amateur dramatics and swimming clubs. After Carreras moved out in 1961, the building was stripped of all its Egyptian decoration. The two giant black cats were relocated to Carreras factories in Jamaica and Essex, and a solar disc of the sun god Ra was removed. The factory was then used

Exterior view of the Carreras cigarette factory, Mornington Crescent, as it appears today. Thiis 1928 art deco building was converted to offices in 1996.

by the Greater London Council, but restored by new, Taiwanese owners in the late 1990s. The cats were returned to their proper place, jealously guarding the entrance portal to Camden.

While Bedford New Town was slowly dismembered over several decades, Agar Town, another abortive fringe Camden neighbourhood, was abruptly erased. Built piecemeal on small plots of land that had been part of Sir William Agar's country estate on the edge of London, Agar Town was notorious by the mid-nineteenth century for its filthy conditions. It was a working-class enclave with just a handful of streets, houses in varying states of repair, some self-built. It suffered from a complete lack of facilities. The local authority, which was the Vestry of St Pancras, failed to provide sewage, road surfaces or street lighting, and the resulting conditions led to its nickname of 'Ague Town'.[23]

Agar Town was entirely cleared by the Midland Railway in 1866 for coal depots and goods sidings, with the demolition of 4,000 houses and the displacement of perhaps 32,000 people. Today, the Elm Village estate occupies its footprint, and there is no trace of the lost streets. However, Agar Town is indirectly remembered in Camden through a blue plaque above No. 256 Camden High Street. This is a memorial to bare-knuckle boxer Tom Sayers, who died there in 1856 at the age of thirty-nine.

Sayers actually lived at what is now No. 51 Camden Street, nearby, and had come to visit his friend John Mensley who lived over his boot-blacking factory on the High Street. Unfortunately, Sayers was taken ill and never left, probably killed by the diabetes that afflicted him. Sayers had been one of the most popular and fêted sportsmen of his time, in an era when boxing was extraordinarily brutal. He fought bare-knuckled, before Queensberry Rules had been introduced, and was only defeated once. He reached the peak of his fame when he drew with American John Heenan in a 42-round match that lasted 2 hours and 20 minutes and left Heenan with a broken hand and Sayers with, apparently, a broken arm. The fight was a sensation, eagerly followed by everyone from

'Paradise-row, Agar-town', in George Godwin, with illustrations by John Brown, *London Shadows: A Glance at the 'Homes' of the Thousands*, Routledge, 1854.

Queen Victoria downwards. It was his last fight, and he retired on the proceeds of a public subscription.

Born in Brighton, Sayers later moved to Agar Town where he worked as a bricklayer, helping to build King's Cross Station. His funeral procession, modelled on that of the Duke of Wellington, attracted a crowd of 100,000 people as the cortege passed through Camden to Highgate Cemetery with his mastiff, an enormous dog called Lion, sitting in pride of place in the lead carriage. A life-size stone version of Lion lies in front of Sayers's Highgate tomb.

Much of George Gissing's 1891 novel *New Grub Street* is set in poor lodgings on the fringes of Camden, next to the railway sidings where Agar Town once was. St Paul's Crescent, between Camden Square and Agar Grove, is still a corner that is very easy to miss. It is cut off to the south by the extraordinarily complex railway junctions behind King's Cross – North London cut adrift, streets of Victorian flats floating in unidentified urban space. George Gissing found it the perfect setting for the endless struggles of Marian Yule and her father Alfred to make a living as hack writers, in 'the obscurity of Camden Road'. Marian spends her days working desperately in the British Museum Reading Room, returning 'faint with weariness and hunger' to a small house on St Paul's Crescent. 'The gloom of a cold and stormy September was doubly wretched in that house on the far borders of Camden Town', wrote Gissing.[24]

Spiritualism and Free Love

While Camden was a place of bad housing and poor conditions, its housing was to prove its salvation too. Many Victorian terraces were demolished in the post-war decades – those that survived were appreciated anew by middle-classes arrivals. The process of change, driving the upturn in Camden's fortunes from the mid-1960s, built on a tradition of artists and writers going back to Rimbaud and Verlaine. By the late nineteenth century Camden was increasingly linked with esoteric thinking and alternative living.

At No. 23 Fitzroy Road, a plaque commemorates W. B. Yeats. Both William and his brother Jack lived in Primrose Hill as children, after the family moved to London from Dublin as their father, John Butler Yeats, pursued his career as a painter. When the boys were in their teens they returned to Dublin, but were back in London by 1887 by which time William's interests were developing fast. He had already been involved in founding the Dublin branch of the Hermetic Order of the Golden Dawn, an organisation surrounded with Masonic-style rituals, set up to study the paranormal and the occult. Meanwhile, Jack, who was a distinguished Expressionist painter, won the newly independent Irish Republic's first Olympic medal, a silver awarded at the 1924 Paris Games. As the Olympics still included a cultural competition, it was for a painting.

Much of early twentieth-century literary society was drawn into the spiritualist movement, from Arnold Bennett to Bram Stoker and of course perpetual troublemaker Aleister Crowley – all of whom belonged to the Hermetic Order of the Golden Dawn, an occult revival organisation founded in the 1880s. Camden still contains evidence of the wave of late Victorian and Edwardian obsession with spiritualism, of which the Golden Dawn was just one manifestation. Rochester Square, off Camden Road, was built over in the mid-nineteenth century, its centre filled with houses. In 1926 the Rochester Square Spiritualist Temple was added, a low key Arts and Crafts building with a foundation stone laid by Arthur Conan Doyle, who was a leading spiritualist. He had dabbled in séances and conducted psychic experiments early in his life, but returned to spiritualism looking for solace after the First World War, in which his son died. He believed the spirit world was a 'New Revelation' and often lectured on the subject. His lesser known fictional hero, the volatile Professor Challenger, who first appeared in *The Lost World*, was sent on a spiritualist quest in *The Land of Mist*, published in 1926.

Ninety years later the temple is still operating, run by the Spiritualist National Union, whose motto is 'Light, Nature, Truth'. It declares confidently that 'The Temple has remained open ever since and we are aiming to keep it open until the end of the world and maybe one day longer'.[26] However, the building is looking the worse for wear, and while closed for repairs in 2014 was squatted by a group called the Rainbow Family of Living Light, 'artists, musicians, masseurs and poets' looking for a 'spiritual refuge'.[27] Mornington Terrace, almost on top of the mainline railway cutting, was home to the smokiest houses in Camden. In one of these, at No. 12, H. G. Wells spent two years as part of an unorthodox progression from the heights of Primrose Hill to the social borderland of the railway fringe. Originally from Bromley, Wells was a science teacher at Henley House School in Kilburn. In 1891 he moved to Fitzroy Road to lodge with his aunt. Soon he married his cousin, Isabel. Four years later he left her, moving to No. 12 Mornington Terrace (then called Mornington Road) with one of his students, Amy Robbins. In this house he wrote both *The Time Machine* and *The Island of Dr Moreau*. Primrose Hill also plays an important role in his most famous book, *The War of the Worlds*, the location for the final defeat of the Martian invasion. The book's narrator witnesses the 'The tattered red shreds of flesh that dripped down upon the overturned seats on the summit of Primrose Hill',[28] the aftermath of the microbes that have destroyed the terrifying Martian war machines.

This scandal was just the beginning. He and Amy (later known as Jane) married, but their marriage was open. With Jane's knowledge and consent, Wells had a series of affairs with some of the most remarkable women of their time, including author Elizabeth von Armin; the Dutch socialist travel writer Odette Keun; Moura Budberg, Russian double agent and former lover of Maxim Gorky; and American birth-control pioneer Margaret Sanger. He had a son with the writer Rebecca West, and a daughter with Amber Reeves, twenty years his junior, a feminist writer whose parents were his friends. A dumpy man with a large moustache, Wells made an unlikely international lover. Contemporaries caricatured him as a womaniser, but his various relationships all seem to have been based on strong mutual attraction.

Poet Charlotte Mew, who lived on Delancey Street in the 1920s, is a semi-forgotten figure, having suffered from severe depression and committed suicide in 1928. She grew up in Bloomsbury, plagued by family disasters. Three of her sisters died young and two more were sent to institutions. She and her surviving sister made a pact never to marry, to avoid passing on the mental illness to which they believed they were prone. In fact, Charlotte, her hair cut short and dressed in masculine clothes, was almost certainly lesbian in an era when the possibility was barely recognised. Her poetry, admired by Thomas Hardy and Virginia Woolf among others, is haunted by unidentified lovers.

The Mornington Crescent end of Camden had been home to artists and writers for longer. George Macdonald lived on Albert Street in the 1860s. Author of *Lilith*, *Sir Gibbie* and *The Princess and the Goblin*, he was a Scottish theologian who wrote early fantasy novels, influencing J. R. R. Tolkien and in particular C. S. Lewis, who referred to him as his 'master'. Macdonald was friends with Lewis Carroll, and *Alice in Wonderland* was published at his persuasion after it impressed his children. He was part of the Victorian literary establishment, mixing with everyone from Dickens and Tennyson to Longfellow and Whitman. Success took him far from Camden, socially at least, and he ultimately left for a house designed especially for him, in Sussex.

George Cruikshank, the most popular cartoonist of his age, lived at No. 48 Mornington Place (now No. 263 Hampstead Road) for 28 years from 1850. Cruikshank, now particularly remembered for his excoriating political caricatures of the dissolute Prince Regent and for his illustrations to *Oliver Twist*, was plagued by debt. His career followed peculiar paths. He conducted a lengthy feud with Charles Dickens, became a temperance activist, and formed a volunteer rifle corps known as 'Havelock's Temperance Volunteers' in response to a French invasion scare. His money problems were not helped by his unusual domestic arrangements. His first wife Mary had died in 1849, and within two years he had married his second wife, Eliza. However, he also had eleven children with his maid Adelaide

Attree, who lived in a flat around the corner where Cruikshank also had his studio. Here he lived a parallel life as 'Robert Archibold', his children all receiving the invented surname. Meanwhile the year before Cruikshank moved in, Alfred Tennyson, lodging on the same street at No. 25 Mornington Place, left the only complete manuscript of his epic poem *In Memoriam* in a cupboard, and had to send devotee and fellow poet Coventry Patmore to retrieve it.

Painting Camden's Secrets

The Camden Town Group was active as a collective for three years, between 1911 and 1914. Only Walter Sickert, the group's leading member, is widely known, leaving a powerful impression on the collective consciousness of dark lodging-house interiors and equally gloomy lives. However, the remainder of the group, which included as many as sixteen painters, left a distinctive record of everyday life in London, particularly Camden. A contemporary critic commented that, 'Whatever else these young artists may or may not be doing, they are treating art as if it had something to do with contemporary life. They paint music halls, hansom cabs, coster girls, back gardens and even back bedrooms'.[29]

Walter Sickert, influenced by Degas, was a long-standing, self-described 'London Impressionist'. As far back as 1889 he had described London as 'the most wonderful and complex city in the world,'[30] dedicating himself to doing it justice. A contemporary critic described his translation of French art into a London context as turning 'absinthe into beer'. He had lived in Camden before, with a studio in Robert Street off Cumberland Market, during the 1880s and 1890s before leaving to spend seven years in Dieppe. During this first period in Camden he painted lodging-house and music-hall pictures (discussed in Chapter 1). On his return in 1905 he moved around studios before settling in Mornington Crescent.

The Camden Town Group was founded in the wake of Roger Fry's notorious *Manet and the Post-Impressionists* exhibition at the Grafton Gallery, Mayfair, in 1910, which shocked the public and coined the collective description for the works on show by Cézanne, Gauguin, Matisse, Seurat and van Gogh. Sickert and a number of younger painters, exposed for the first time to unstable lines and wild colours, set up the group in response.

Apart from Sickert, the group's core members were Robert Bevan, Harold Gilman, Charles Ginner and Spencer Gore. The Group was deliberately all-male. Its full membership included artists such as Duncan Grant and Wyndham Lewis, who were only peripherally connected to the Camden style. Mornington Crescent was the epicentre, with Sickert at No. 6 Mornington Crescent and Gore lodging on the same street, while Bevan lived a few minutes' walk away in Cumberland Market.

The Camden Town Group produced many London works, including a series of textured Camden pictures which, at their best, are deeply atmospheric. The Camden Town genre they created was based on small pictures of unassuming subjects, often nudes lying on brass beds in down-at-heel Camden back rooms. Alongside Sickert, Spencer Gore was the pick of the painters, and the two visited the music halls together. When Gore was able to extract himself from Camden interiors and paint the streets, his colours broke free too. His *Nearing Euston Station* from 1911 shows red and yellow advertisements splashed on muddy mauve railway ironwork, as a steam train passes through the Camden cutting; his *Mornington Crescent* from the same year paints the deep ox-blood façade of the tube station as a bright beacon in a leafy square. Gilman, who painted his housekeeper Mrs Mounter, and Ginner, who also painted London streets, were lesser lights. Iain Sinclair describes the latter as 'Van Gogh on Prozac',[31] and it is true that they lacked the true tonal derangement of their continental contemporaries.

Three group shows were held, but the divergent styles of Sickert and his colleagues caused friction, particularly their attitudes to colour. Gilman moved away from Sickert's influence, and Wyndham Lewis later claimed that 'he would look over in the

Spencer Gore, *From a Window in the Hampstead Road*. Oil on canvas, 1911.
Sotheby's, London.

direction of Sickert's studio, and a slight shudder would convulse him as he thought of the little brown worm of paint wriggling out on to the palette'.[32] Gilman and Ginner re-launched themselves as 'New Realists'. Sickert, who enjoyed a controversy, waded in with an article attacking their style: 'The Thickest Painters in London'.

The group came to a sudden end with the premature death of Gore at the age of thirty-five, from pneumonia. Gilman, Ginner and Bevan formed a successor collective, the Cumberland Market Group, based in Bevan's studio at No. 49 Cumberland Market. Their 'New Realist' agenda aimed to reign in what they saw as Impressionist excess, focusing on natural observation of the city. Bevan's paintings of the Cumberland Market district, now completely rebuilt, show the wide, wintry spaces of the underused market square, covered carts parked in a line, horses with their heads deep in their nosebags. However, Bevan had a foot in both camps, and also formed the new London Group with Sickert, a more avant-garde project that included the sculptors Jacob Epstein and Henri Gaudier-Brzeska and which, remarkably, still exists.

The Cumberland Market Group folded in tragic circumstances when Charles Ginner returned from military service in the First World War with Spanish influenza. He was looked after by Harold Gilman, who caught the disease and died – a victim of the global epidemic that claimed more lives than the war that had just ended.

The artists of Camden Town, in their various formations, left a legacy of documentation which gave their early twentieth-century neighbourhoods an identity of its own. For the first time an artistic conception of Camden was at large, alongside the sometimes dark and relentless reality. Re-appropriation by new arrivals was to prove a defining characteristic of modern Camden. If they have a twenty-first-century successor, it is surely Frank Auerbach, whose life's work takes the immediate surroundings of Mornington Crescent as its main subject. Auerbach came to Britain on the *Kindertransport* in 1939, escaping Germany and the Holocaust, in which his parents died. His artistic life began at Borough Polytechnic in the late 1940s, where he was taught by the Vorticist painter David

Bomberg. He had learned his skills from Walter Sickert, who lived feet away from where Auerbach now works.

Auerbach's obsessive examination of a small area of south Camden began in the post-war years, when the streets and the people were marked by the Blitz. As he saw it, 'London looked marvellous in those days. There were endless vistas in the gaps between buildings, and the sight of houses sheared away by explosions was very dramatic'.[33] He first painted the Carreras building in 1961, depicting it in impasto gouts of black, white and grey. The focus of his painting is the Hampstead Road in front of the factory, reflecting shiny white and wet, with the factory a featureless grey presence dominating the traffic. There is no trace of exoticism, and the Black Cat Factory has been comprehensively assimilated into heavy, drab, post-war London.

Auerbach saw something special in what most dismissed as depressing and drab, and has produced canvas after canvas documenting the immediate neighbourhood of Mornington Crescent where it meets Hampstead Road. His paintings feature the curved terrace of the crescent, the tube station and, most frequently, the view from the junction of the three Ampthill Estate towers, topped in child's crayon shades of red, yellow and blue. 'The closer one is to something, the more likely it is to be beautiful', he says.[34] He has painted from the same Camden studio for fifty years, where he lives an ascetic existence, spending as much time as possible laying down thick, choppy layers of paint. Three evenings a week he sees his wife, and he takes one day off a year. He is regarded by many as Britain's greatest living painter.

Gentrification

The Survey of London, written in 1952, described Camden's houses as 'not distinguished by sufficient architectural character to merit description', and added that many of the properties were dilapidated.[35] At the time, Camden epitomised the tired, crowded bombed inner city that many were desperate to escape. Accounts from the time are not enthusiastic.

Dylan Thomas lived with his wife Caitlin and their three children at No. 54 Delancey Street, a basement flat bought for him by his obsessed patron, Margaret Taylor, who lived nearby with her husband, historian A. J. P Taylor. They spent only three months there from October 1951 until leaving for a US lecture tour in January 1952. Thomas was not impressed, writing of 'our new London house of horror on bus and night lorry route and opposite railway bridge and shunting station'.[36] However, a new generation saw things differently. Camden contained a comprehensive typology of Victoria houses, from double bay fronts to terraces. On Parkway, for example, houses from around 1820 are 'a box of rooms' – very simple with a single room on each floor, parquet floors, cream walls, plain surfaces and maybe a marble mantelpiece as the only decoration.[37] Author Colin MacInnes lived in the adjoining Regent's Park Terrace in the 1940s, as did Terence Conran, before either became famous and before it was the kind of place famous people lived. From the 1960s, however, this relatively short stretch of houses, usefully screened from passers-by, became the location of choice for successful figures in science and the arts, including the poet Louis MacNeice, novelist V. S. Pritchett and philosopher A. J. Ayer, statistician Claus Moser, actress Judi Dench and Conran's son Jasper. In the intervening period, gentrification had come to Camden.

Camden was hot territory for recolonisation of the war-battered inner city by those who spotted cheap property and convenient locations. There was also, of course, money both old and new, from family fortunes as well as spectacular careers. Coined in 1964 by the sociologist Ruth Glass at University College London, a short hop from Camden Town, the term 'gentrification' described the social changes she had observed in Georgian and Victorian inner London. First observed in Canonbury, it spread next to Camden and Primrose Hill, and reached Kentish Town, Notting Hill and Holland Park during the 1960s. The following decade, gentrification moved south of the river. These areas had several factors in common – they were well-equipped with two- and three-storey houses, suitable for families, and were close to already established middle-class areas. Young professionals simply moved into houses in the adjoining neighbourhood, which were well-built but in need of renovation. There was always somewhere to move next: 'If the squares have now been priced out of reach, there always remains the bijou artisans' cottage.'[38]

Gloucester Crescent is quintessential gentrified Camden, only a block away from the High Street but entirely out of sight, and even now radiating a certain moneyed, bohemian charm. Despite being close to the railway, Gloucester Crescent was where several of the more highbrow stars of the 1960s cultural boom moved with the proceeds of their fame. It was, and to some extent still is, inhabited by a selection of authors, filmmakers, journalists and literary types including Peter Blake, Alan Bennett, Susannah Clapp, Jonathan Miller, Deborah Moggach, Karel Reisz and Claire Tomalin.

Around the corner in Albert Street, Beryl Bainbridge lived chaotically, a stuffed water buffalo called Eric installed in her hall to greet visitors. Bainbridge was part of an Albert Street crowd that included the actor Denholm Elliott. Her domestic arrangements, bohemian to a fault, recall those of George Cruikshank a century earlier. She kept a separate flat nearby where she conducted a long-term affair with Colin Haycraft, her publisher at Duckworth (based close by in the former Collard & Collard rotunda on Oval Road). She was good friends with Haycraft's wife Anna (the novelist Alice Thomas Ellis) – all the more surprising given Anna's traumatic affair with Bainbridge's first husband.

Camden-set film *Withnail and I* reflects much of the ambiance of late 1960s Camden Town, centred on Albert Street, just before gentrification hits the street. Writer and director Bruce Robinson was at drama school when, in 1967, he moved into an Albert Street house that had been bought by classmate Lord David Dundas, heir to the Marquess of Zetland, a student with more money than most. The flat became a student squat, and while Dundas soon had enough and bought himself another flat in Hampstead, his friends continued to live on Albert Street, enjoying Guinness for breakfast, wine for lunch and joints for tea.

By 1969 only Robinson and fellow student Vivian MacKerrell were left at Albert Street, their payments frozen, enduring a bitterly cold winter, living off pilchards, raisins and turnips scavenged from the market. Their life on the margins is portrayed in the opening scenes of *Withnail and I*. The landlord of the Spread Eagle, also on Albert Street, was the model for the drunken, pheasant-loving patron at the film's Crow & Crown pub.

The incestuous atmosphere of literary Camden is represented in Nina Stibbe's Gloucester Crescent diaries. In the early 1980s Stibbe nannied for Mary-Kay Wilmers, editor and proprietor of the *London Review of Books*, at No. 55 Gloucester Crescent, and her letters to her sister reporting on the street's inhabitants were a surprise success when published in 2013. It is populated by household names who wander in and out of each other's houses eating mashed potato and complaining about Arsenal.

Stibbe's Gloucester Crescent room had previously belonged to larger-than-life jazz musician George Melly, and it was Melly who had already spotted the comic potential of the Crescent. He wrote captions for a series of cartoons by Mark Boxer, 'The String-Alongs'. These were published in the *Listener* from 1969 and featured a media couple, Simon and Joanna String-Along, who had just moved to a house 'north of the park' and blew with the winds of fashion. The String-Alongs identified and satirised a new group of left-liberal, arts and media people, with a status in society affirmed in the aftermath of the 1960s counter cultural change. A sample scene has a mother in bob, beads and dark-rimmed glasses, telling her son 'Don't worry: your father and I think spelling is elitist'. The setting was in fact Gloucester Crescent, where inspiration came not least from Mary-Kay Wilmers, who was then married to film director Stephen Frears and working at the *Listener*.

Alan Bennett may have been the first author to write about the gentrification or 'knocking through' happening around him in Camden. After *Beyond the Fringe ended*, his first project was a television sketch comedy called *On the Margin*, shown in 1966. The series was thought lost for years, having been deleted by the BBC, but a copy turned up in 2014. One of the sketches was called 'Streets Ahead: Life and Times in NW1' and involved competitive Camden couples. It is said to have inspired Boxer and Melly. Bennett described both the comedy and the problem of the change brought by new arrivals, such as himself, as being 'the difference between our social position and our social obligations'.[39] The incomers lived parallel existences, owing nothing to the place around them.

The Primrose Path

Alan Bennett moved up to Primrose Hill in the 2000s, escaping the 'drunks, drug-dealers, snogging by the wall, and the stop-and-search' of Camden.[40] Kingsley Amis's 1990 novel *The Folks That Live on the Hill* is set in a very thinly disguised Primrose Hill, seen through a typically jaded lens. It is occupied by incestuous divorcees who spend their time reading the *Mail*, taking downers and drinking Cinzano. Their surroundings include 'a bistro where the man shouted at the customers' and 'the post office, or rather the post-office-cum-stationer's-cum-newsagent's-cum-tobacconists-confectioner's-delicatessen-cum-video-library-cum-(from next week)-dry-cleaning establishment'.[41] Primrose Hill was in transition, its heyday already twenty years in the past, and had become as Conservative-voting and conventional a neighbourhood as everywhere colonised by the financially successful.

Primrose Hill is a self-contained neighbourhood, a respectable version of Camden Town, within easy reach of the High Street but distinctly separate. Charles Booth's social survey of 1898 described it as 'The Island' – 'dull, unexciting' but 'highly respectable'.[42] It remains all of these things, a peculiarly isolated patch of streets hugged tight by the railway. To the north and the east the main line to Euston and the old railway lands, now occupied by Morrisons and its giant car park, frustrate attempts to enter. From this side, the only portal is the hidden footbridge over the railway from Chalk Farm. The south and west are cushioned by the slopes of Primrose Hill itself, dropping away towards Regent's Park. The Regent's Canal places a boundary across the two streets shared with Camden. The result is a place that is often suspended in slightly eerie stillness. It was these characteristics that ensured it was one of the first areas of Victorian inner London to be gentrified during the 1960s, and twenty-first-century Primrose Hill is now a resort of the moneyed. However, despite its respectability it has never been entirely conventional.

Before development Primrose Hill was countryside west of Chalk Farm Road (then called Pancras Vale). The only street was Primrose Vale, now Regent's Park Road, which connected Pancras Vale to the summit of the hill. The Chalk Farm Tavern was located halfway along at the heart of modern Primrose Hill, on a site that is now No. 89 Regent's Park Road. Almost all of the Primrose Hill we see today, developed on Lord Southampton's land, was complete by the 1870s. Primrose Hill Studios, tucked in the centre of the block behind Fitzroy Road, was built in 1877 as accommodation for artists. It has housed a remarkable range of painters, including Arthur Rackham and John William Waterhouse during the first decade of the twentieth century, both fully immersed in folklore and classical myth among the stuccoed Primrose Hill terraces. Henry Wood, conductor and founder of the Proms, lived there too, and more recently post-war painters Patrick Caulfield and John Hoyland were based in the studios.

At the southern end of Primrose Hill, the painter William Roberts lived in St Mark's Crescent after the Second World War. One of the original Vorticists, Roberts documented domestic London scenes such as the interior of a barber's shop, or local events including Hampstead Fair, in a characteristically epic, modernist style. His reputation as a recluse in the post-war years seems to have come mostly from spending his time with his wife in Primrose Hill.

However, it was possible to run a career in the public eye from St Mark's Crescent. During the same period, the historian A. J. P. Taylor lived next-door to Roberts, where he campaigned for CND and developed his reputation as the 'people's historian', challenging 'great man' theories of history in works such as *The Origins of the Second World War*.

Sylvia Plath and Ted Hughes, then in their twenties, first lived together in Primrose Hill, at No. 3 Chalcot Square where they moved in 1959. Plath, from Boston, met Hughes at Cambridge, where she had come on a Fulbright scholarship. Four months later they married. She was delighted by her first impressions of London, from the policemen to the zoo, and loved Primrose Hill despite finding it 'quite slummy'. However, her life became infamously dark, and the bright pink, three-storey terrace in Chalcot Square is where her marriage started to fall apart.

The couple left London to spend an ill-advised year in the Devon village of North Tawton. It was while they were in temporary exile that Hughes began an affair with Assia Wevill, who had rented No. 3 Chalcot Square with her husband, David. In her poem, 'Parliament Hill Fields', Plath looks down on Camden and Kentish Town from the edge of the Hampstead Ridge where 'the tumulus, even at noon, guards its black shadow',[43] a threatening, ancient presence perched high above the terraces. Later, after she and Hughes had separated, she came back to Primrose Hill with her two children, living only a street away in the top floor flat at No. 23 Fitzroy Road, the former home of W. B. and J. B. Yeats. Plath wrote her novel, *The Bell Jar*, in the Fitzroy Road flat, anatomising the depression that would lead to her suicide. She killed herself there in February 1963. Much later, in 2010, Ted Hughes published 'Last Letter' in which he describes how he slept with a lover on the night of her suicide, and imagines seeing Sylvia Plath in the snowy winter streets 'just turning / Out of Fitzroy Road, crossing over / Between the heaped up banks of dirty sugar'.[44]

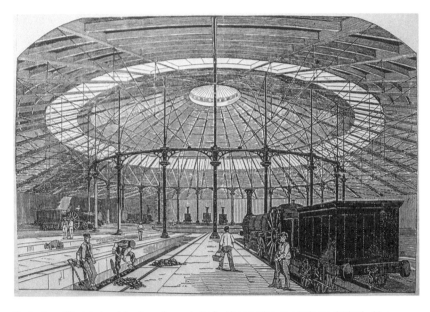

Illustration of the interior of the Roundhouse in its first incarnation, as a train repair shed with a central turntable, 1847.

Chapter 5 **From Underground to Overground**

The wide-hipped Roundhouse, with its low, conical roof, looks like a brick circus-top pitched beside the Chalk Farm Road. Its form is instantly recognisable as an alternative Albert Hall, the home of experimental performance and the symbol of Camden's special claim to cultural significance.

Despite appearances the Roundhouse did not begin life as a place of entertainment, but as a train repair shed, with a design so bespoke that within ten years it was redundant. Round buildings are usually associated with the mysterious and the ancient – Templar churches and Celtic dwelling houses – rather than working structures, but the shape was a logical response to the need to house a very large railway turntable. It was designed by Robert Dockray, a Quaker engineer working for railway pioneer Robert Stephenson, chief engineer of the London and Birmingham Railway. Dockray's building housed repair bays with sunken inspection pits, like a car repair workshop, arranged around a turntable so that engines could be shunted in, repaired and turned back out again. The Roundhouse had twenty-three bays between twenty-four cast iron columns holding up the roof. It opened in 1847, but locomotive design advanced rapidly and trains soon became too long to fit the shed. The Roundhouse was rendered obsolete, and it took a century for it to discover a new purpose.

By the 1860s it had been hired by furniture movers Pickfords, then used as a potato and corn warehouse. In 1869 W. A. Gilbey, importers of wine and distillers of gin, converted the building into a secure, bonded warehouse for their stock, removing most of the railway fittings. Gilbey's occupied the Roundhouse for ninety-four years as part of their sprawling Camden headquarters. It was only when the company eventually moved out in 1963 that the Roundhouse began to shape Camden in a different way.

The Roundhouse Revival

By the time Gilbey's vacated the Roundhouse, Camden Town had become, along with other fashionable districts such as Chelsea and Notting Hill, a favoured place for art students and a budding centre of the new underground. Unlike the more tailored King's Road, Camden belonged, according to 1960s kingpin Barry Miles, to 'the grubby, revolutionary hippies'.[1] It was cheap but relatively central, and the first stirrings could be detected of a cultural upheaval that would define the era, and change perceptions of Camden entirely.

The Roundhouse Trust acquired the building's freehold in 1963, donated by the socialist tycoon Louis Mintz who approved of plans for a new, democratic arts space. Playwright and campaigner Arnold Wesker took charge as artistic director, declaring the state of the arts in Britain 'a mean joke'. His lobbying had led the Trades Union Congress to pass Resolution 42, supporting an inquiry into the arts, and the Roundhouse was therefore renamed Centre 42. Wesker planned a new arts venue for the people, designed to confront cultural snobbery and bring the arts into everyday life. Prime Minister Harold Wilson hosted a tea party to raise funds.

The initial plan was to convert the circular space into a theatre, with facilities in the surrounding spaces such as film editing suites. However, the acoustics were not ideal, with an echo that generations of designers have since struggled to contain, while the cast iron pillars cut inconveniently across the sightlines. The space worked best for events that did away with the separation between performers and their audience – exactly the sort of happening for which the Roundhouse was shortly to become famous.

ALL NIGHT RAVE to launch new underground newspaper 'INTERNATIONAL TIMES' it the Soft Machine; the Pink Floyd; steel bands STRIP - TRIPS - HAPPENING MOVIE - POP - OP - COSTUME MASQUE - DRAG BALL bring your own poison, bring Flowers & gass filled balloons SurPRIZE for Shortest & Barest at... THE ROUND HOUSE* opp.chalk farm underground SAT. 15th OCT 11 P.M. onwards. advance tickets 5/- from INDICA better books; Dobells Record Shop. GRANNIE TAKE A TRIP Mandarin Book Shops at... Nottinghill gate & Swiss Cottage, or Compulsory donations of 10/- at door.

Poster advertising an all-night rave to launch the *International Times* on 15 October 1966. This was the opening event for the Roundhouse's new role as an alternative arts venue.

The launch party for quintessential 1960s publication the *International Times* (known as the *IT*, founded by London's counterculture lynchpins Barry Miles and John 'Hoppy' Hopkins) opened the new venue in October 1966. The Roundhouse was 'old, wet, filthy with minimal lighting, a rickety balcony and only two toilets', but nevertheless the event sold out.[2] Hand-lettered posters advertised an 'All Night Rave' headlined by Pink Floyd and Soft Machine. One version instructed attendees to 'bring your own poison & flowers & gass-filled [*sic*] balloons & submarine & rocket ship & candy & striped boxes & ladders & paint & flutes & feet & ladders & locomotives & madness & autumn & blowlamps'. Guests were ceremonially handed a sugar-cube at the door, although this turned out to contain only sugar. There was a 6-foot high green jelly as a centrepiece, later apparently run over by Pink Floyd's van. Paul McCartney turned up dressed as a sheikh. Marianne Faithfull, dressed as a nun, won the 'shortest and barest' competition. Soft Machine guitarist Daevid Allen later stoked the legend that grew around the party, describing the evening as 'One of the most revolutionary events in the history of English alternative music and thinking'.[3] It was ground-breaking, chaotic and bizarre, and a sign of things to come at the Roundhouse.

UFO Lands in Camden

The cultural changes simmering through the 1960s came to the boil in Camden when the UFO club came to the Roundhouse. By late 1966 this new all-nighter, in the Blarney Club, a basement under a cinema on Tottenham Court Road, was the sensation of the moment. It was sound-tracked by house bands Pink Floyd, Soft Machine and the Crazy World of Arthur Brown, and the bill featured most of the rest of the British underground. UFO was a phenomenon, attracting bigger and bigger crowds until the cramped basement became impossibly full. It also attracted the attention of the press and the police. The papers sent in journalists 'undercover' who claimed to have spotted people 'smoking joss-sticks'. After just six months the police told the venue to choose between UFO and its licence, and the club was kicked out.

Despite an offer of a West End theatre, UFO chose instead to relocate to the Roundhouse, 'a magnificently decaying brick hulk on the edge of the railway lands', according to organiser Joe Boyd.[4] It proved a bad business decision. Boyd, producer of Fairport Convention and the Incredible String Band among others, had set up UFO in partnership with 'Hoppy' Hopkins. In July 1967 the innocence around the underground in London came to an abrupt end when Hoppy was sentenced, vindictively, to nine months in Wormwood Scrubs for possessing cannabis.

Without Hoppy, UFO fell apart. The club ran for only eight weekends at the Roundhouse before vanishing into a financial black hole – but these were no ordinary weekends. From the ground-breaking psychedelic posters of Hapshash and the Coloured Coat (the collective identity of designers Michael English and Nigel Waymouth) to the Boyle Family's ground-breaking light shows, UFO encapsulated the defining aesthetic of its time with the help of free-flowing LSD, supplied by a fat, German dealer called Manfred. The result was an entirely new experience for young audiences, transporting them to new destinations. The Third Ear Band claimed to have 'drifted into a completely different dimension' while playing on stage at UFO, unintentionally pausing time while playing a song called 'Druid'.

The Roundhouse was vast compared to Tottenham Court Road. Although bands such as Jeff Beck, Pink Floyd, Pretty Things and Tomorrow played for relatively small fees, the venue sucked up funds. It needed more staff on the many doors, and bigger crowds to fill the cavernous space. Each night half the take was reserved for underground causes, particularly IT and the charity Release, which supplied bust funds to people arrested for possession.

Camden turned out to be less relaxed than the West End about the new, long-haired crowds. Before the Roundhouse, there was no particular reason for outsiders to visit an unexceptional, solidly working-class neighbourhood. The Saturday night drinking culture of industrial Camden was at odds with the acid-soaked Roundhouse happenings, and skinheads quickly took note of the beaded-up long-hairs on their patch. Hippies making their way along Chalk Farm Road were attacked, and on one occasion a gang even burst through the Roundhouse fire doors, randomly punching audience members inside. Organised crime took an interest; Barry Miles was robbed of his rather insubstantial takings by men armed with pickaxe handles and ammonia, who ambushed him in the doorway of his house at the conclusion of one weekend.

The takings stayed down, partly because of the outlay on extra security after these incidents. Naturally, the Roundhouse hired the most unconventional bouncers they could find, paying Michael X and his Black Nationalist heavies to run the door. Joe Boyd explains that, despite their black-clad menace and karate skills 'they could not have been gentler souls'.[5] However, there was definitely another side to Michael X, whose precarious and sinister life led, via extortion charges, communes and mysterious fires, to his execution for murder in 1975 in Trinidad.

In slightly less terrifying ways, others were soon heading for the exit. One of UFO's theme songs was 'Granny Takes a Trip' by the Purple Gang, with lead singer Pete 'Lucifer' Walker. The band was short-lived because Walker left to become initiated as a warlock (the BBC, who banned the single, were reported to have said that 'a band that boasts a warlock for a singer will not be tolerated by any decent society'). Jack Bracelin, a Wiccan High Priest who ran Five Acre Lights at UFO, gave up light shows to run a nudist club. UFO closed in September 1967, sunk by its losses, but it left behind many of the most potent and influential images of the era.

The Avant-garde on Chalk Farm Road

But the Roundhouse continued to occupy centre stage. In 1968 a procession of the biggest bands of the time played the rotunda, from Jefferson Airplane to Jimi Hendrix and Hawkwind to the Who. UFO's one-time rival, the Middle Earth club, moved to the Roundhouse in late 1968 having been forced out of its Covent Garden home. It lasted long enough to host one of only two British appearances by the Doors, as well as Led Zeppelin's first show. The Beatles were involved from early on, George Harrison and Paul McCartney staging a 1966 event called Carnival of Light, where experimental sounds accompanied light shows on 60-foot screens. For the event the press reported that McCartney had 'recorded a tape of electronic noises – known as music in some circles'.[6] The Beatles did indeed record a live, fourteen-minute experimental track, 'Carnival of Light', at the Million Volt Sound and Light Rave back at the Roundhouse the following year, which has become notorious for having never been released. The Jimi Hendrix Experience played at the same event and someone stole Hendrix's Stratocaster, running away with it up Haverstock Hill.

The Beatles had worked on both events with Delia Derbyshire, pioneer of electronic music at the BBC Radiophonic Workshop. Here she famously created the *Doctor Who* theme music, part of a body of work that created an entirely new sound. She was also based in Camden, setting up the Kaleidophon studio at 281–283 Camden High Street in the late 1960s with Workshop colleague Brian Hodgson (the man behind the sound of the Daleks), and musician and engineer David Vorhaus. At Kaleidophon Derbyshire made music that stretched beyond the confines of her job at the BBC – for theatre, and as the band White Noise with Hodgson and Vorhaus. Their 1969 album *An Electric Storm* used a prototype, home-made synthesiser, as well as tape sampling and manipulation, and was some distance ahead of its time, influencing a long line of later musicians. As Derbyshire said in an interview during the Kaleidophon years, 'Welcome to the world of the Frequency Shifter, Signal Generator and Azimuth Co-ordinator'.[7]

The Roundhouse also became known for avant-garde theatre. New international groups who relished the challenges of the unconventional space came to Camden. The kings of alternative

Car crash exhibit at J. G. Ballard's exhibition *Crashed Cars*, sponsored by the Institute for Research in Art and Technology, Robert Street, London, 1970. The wrecked Pontiac illustrates Ballard's assertion that 'the car crash is the most dramatic event we are likely to experience in our entire lives apart from our own deaths'.

performance were New York's Living Theatre, who embraced nakedness and audience confrontation. They often began their performances by sitting in silence for half an hour, attempting to levitate. The Boyle Family set up Sensual Laboratory, and staged *Son et Lumiére for Bodily Functions and Fluids*, in which ECG monitors (measuring heart rate) and EEG monitors (measuring brain activity) were projected onto a screen, sharing the data with the audience from various live activities, from coughing to copulation. Peter Brook staged his experimental *Themes on the Tempest* in 1968, in which the actors swung from scaffolding towers, joined by some onlookers, while Brook himself roamed the auditorium trying to 'mould the audience into a homogeneous personality'.[8] Brook returned with his era-defining, circus-themed production of *A Midsummer Night's Dream*, which transferred briefly from Stratford in 1970. The cast brought no costumes or set, and performed in and around an audience seated on the floor, happily reinventing the production to suit the particular requirements of the Roundhouse. Other famous productions were seen, including Steven Berkoff making his reputation with a black-and-white version of *Metamorphosis*, and Nicol Williamson's *Hamlet*, directed by Tony Richardson, which was acclaimed as the best of his generation.

However, the Roundhouse was not the only Camden venue to enter 1960s legend. The Arts Lab was an influential alternative arts centre, founded in 1967 on Drury Lane where it lasted just two years. Some of those involved set up a successor, the New Arts Lab (also known as the Institute for Research in Art and Technology), based in a disused pharmaceutical factory building on the corner of Hampstead Road and Robert Street, at the southern edge of Camden. From 1969 to 1971 it operated as a theatre, gallery and 'London's Underground Cinema', and achieved lasting notoriety with J. G. Ballard's *Crashed Cars* exhibition. Prefiguring Ballard's novel, *Crash*, the exhibition consisted of three smashed-up cars – an Austin Cambridge, a Mini and a Pontiac. Ballard, who saw the concrete factory space, the nearby estates and the windswept

Hampstead Road as the perfect dystopian setting, declared that: 'The car crash is the most dramatic event we are likely to experience in our entire lives apart from our own deaths'.[9] The show was designed to provoke, and gallery-goers responded by smashing wine glasses and vandalising the cars, urinating on the seats and breaking windscreens. The New Arts Lab building was demolished during the 1970s, and the site is now occupied by the Surma Centre, home of the Bengali Workers' Association.

The End and the Beginning

The film *Withnail & I* documents the end of counterculture almost as soon as it had begun, with drug dealer Danny bemoaning the hippy wigs for sale in Woolworths and concluding that they had 'blown it'. The Centre 42 dream began to fade when Wesker resigned in 1972, upset by the replacement of his production of his own play *The Friends* with *Oh! Calcutta!*, which had on-stage nudity and greater box office appeal. Wesker felt that Centre 42, increasingly obliged to rent out its auditorium to remain afloat, 'had lost both its building and its impetus'.[10] The struggle to keep the Roundhouse financially viable dominated the 1970s. The venue was run increasingly as a theatre space, first by Centre 42 director George Hoskins and then by theatre producer Thelma Holt. Holt commented that when she arrived that 'the Roundhouse, just as it was every Tuesday and Thursday, was in danger of closing'.[11]

Although stability was elusive, productions staged during this period were highly influential, embracing the unlikely shape and dynamics of the space. In 1976 Ken Campbell and Chris Langham, as the Science Fiction Theatre of Liverpool, commandeered the Roundhouse with an anarchic, nine-hour adaptation of Robert Anton Wilson's and Robert Shea's rambling paranoid *The Illuminatus! Trilogy*. The production, called *Illuminatus!*, spanned acid-fuelled conspiracy theory with the aid

Poster for *Illuminatus!*, Roundhouse, 1977.

The Damned perform at the Roundhouse in 1977.

of sets flung together from Camden's junk shops, and became a theatrical legend. Peter Barnes's 1978 production of Ben Jonson's *Bartholomew Fair* also drew attention, merging auditorium and stage, and filling the building with fairground equipment borrowed from Wookey Hole.

A line of future stars passed through Camden. Ben Kingsley played *Hamlet*, Helen Mirren and Bob Hoskins appeared in *The Duchess of Malfi* and comedian Max Wall made a remarkable transition to the conventional stage in *Waiting for Godot*. Oscar James and Mona Hammond broke new ground in *The Black Macbeth*, as the first black actors to play the roles in Britain. And, perhaps confirming Arnold Wesker's suspicions, *Oh! Calcutta!* was the first in a series of rock musicals staged at the Roundhouse, including *Godspell*, *Rock Carmen* and a musical version of *Othello* called *Catch My Soul*.

Throughout this eclectic period the Roundhouse maintained its reputation as a cultural weathervane, hosting the gig that kick-started punk in Britain. On 4 July 1976, the bicentennial of the American Revolution, the Ramones arrived for their first appearance on British soil, supporting the Flamin' Groovies. Struggling to raise interest in the US, they were astonished to find themselves playing to a sold-out Roundhouse. The band had some difficulty acclimatising to an air-conditioning free London during the heatwave of 1976, complaining that 'businessmen were walking down Piccadilly in wife-beater shirts and there were no ice cubes'.[12] However, they made up for it with 'wild sex romps' in the Camden Holiday Inn and by, during the course of their visit, effectively creating the template for punk.

The Roundhouse was soon hosting the US alternative scene with Patti Smith and Talking Heads, and the British punk wave in the form of the Clash, the Damned, the Stranglers and X-Ray Spex. Local and not so local teenagers were inspired by the music and the culture coming out of Camden. Captain Sensible took the No. 68 bus all the way from Croydon to experience a Roundhouse re-education. Local girls Rebecca Hale and Sarah

Rapson, Sixth Formers at Camden School for Girls, renamed themselves Crystal Clear and Vinyl Virgin and hand-produced a fanzine called *More On*. Funded by Joe Strummer, its four issues helped define the DIY punk aesthetic with a series of famous photos taken by the two girls, including a definitive image of Viv Albertine perched open legged on a bar, wearing fishnets. Meanwhile bands from Can to Fairport Convention were happy to play Implosion Sunday nighters for a minimal fee. Only Pink Floyd and the Rolling Stones insisted on market rates.

Despite its cultural significance, the Roundhouse never attracted the long-term funding it needed. When the Arts Council withdrew its subsidy in 1983, the theatre went dark. Ownership passed to the Greater London Council and then Camden Council. A succession of ambitious plans were abandoned, including a new Centre for Black Arts and Drama, an 'Earth Focus' exhibition involving a giant globe, a permanent London home for the Royal Exchange Theatre, Manchester, a shopping centre, an IMAX cinema, and storage for the RIBA architectural drawings collection. Meanwhile, the building became little more than a shell, providing an appealingly derelict location for films such as Richard Stanley's low-budget 1990 cult horror, *Hardware* ('Get ready for an encounter with some seriously heavy metal!') which made the most of the building's distressed state by transforming it into a post-apocalyptic city.

From the point of apparent no-return, the Roundhouse made a remarkable recovery. The venue reopened in 2006, after lengthy refurbishment. It was derelict when, in 1996, it was bought on impulse by Camden resident Torquil Norman, who had made his money through Bluebird Toys and Polly Pocket dolls. He part-funded the restoration, and chaired a trust to raise the rest of the money. Since 2006 the Roundhouse has been a multi-arts venue, more conventional than that envisaged by Wesker and less wildly experimental than its 1960s and 1970s heyday, but finally with a future. It now prioritises work with young people and has featured a wide selection of offerings, including the Royal Shakespeare

Company's epic staging of the entire Shakespeare history cycle in 2008, concerts for the first time since the 1970s, large-scale art installations, and circus performances which are particularly suited to its tent-like atmosphere.

Compendium and the Literary Scene

While the Roundhouse was at the heart of music and performance in the late 1960s and 1970s, it was also a driving force behind London's literary counterculture. Much of what is cherished about the Roundhouse of the 1960s was encapsulated in the Dialectics of Liberation Conference. The two-week intellectual happening was 'a unique gathering to demystify human violence in all its forms. The intellectual equivalent of levitating the Pentagon'.[13] (The latter had famously been attempted in 1967, when counter culture leaders had obtained government agreement to raise the building by three feet, negotiated down from the 300 feet originally requested.)

The conference was organised by anti-psychiatrists R. D. Laing and David Cooper. Laing was becoming a household name for his theories that family dysfunction gave rise to schizophrenia, and global violence such as the Vietnam War was a form of psychosis. The event included a wide selection of speakers from philosopher Herbert Marcuse and poet Allen Ginsberg, to Black Panther leader Stokely Carmichael and Julian Beck of the Living Theatre.

The Congress led to a version intended to be more permanent, the London Anti-University, which briefly ran classes in Shoreditch. At one of these Diana Gravill was persuaded to invest her £2,000 inheritance in founding a bookshop for the times. She and her partner, Nicholas Rochford, opened Compendium in August 1968, trading for more than thirty years until its closure in 2000. It moved from No. 240 Camden High Street to larger premises at No. 234 in the 1970s, where it specialised in politics, poetry, science fiction, comics and the occult.

Stokely Carmichael speaking in support of Black Power at the Dialectics conference, Roundhouse, 1967.

Compendium tapped into the London counterculture bloodline. In 1965 Barry Miles of UFO fame had set up Indica, a West End gallery and bookshop part-funded by Paul McCartney, where John Lennon first met Yoko Ono. It closed in 1970, driven into bankruptcy by the refusal of its customers to conform to bourgeois notions of ownership by paying for books. Many of Indica's staff decamped to Compendium, conferring the mantle of the underground on Camden Town.

Compendium was to become the centre of alternative literary culture in London from the 1970s until the end of the century. It was a cultural centre of weight and significance with staff who knew their business, and with a fiction and poetry selection to rival City Lights, the San Francisco beat bookshop on which Indica had been based. Iain Sinclair described Compendium as 'a giant leap in the mental health of the metropolis; a confirmation of that unitary vision expressed at the 1967 conference'.[14]

The shop was often subject to official attention, not for its stock of Marxist pamphlets but rather the imported US comics by artists such as Robert Crumb, which were usually sexually explicit and generally included some drug-taking for good measure. The police often raided the shop looking for illegal material, foiled on one occasion by poetry and comics manager Nick Kimberley who managed, improbably, to push all his hot stock under the carpet.

Compendium succeeded in making the cultural transition from its high hippie origins to the punk era. By the mid-1970s the Clash were frequenting the shop, and George's Café opposite. They rehearsed in a warehouse at Camden Lock owned by manager Bernie Rhodes, who also used it to sell second-hand jukeboxes, and the cover photo for their debut album was taken in Camden Market. Joe Strummer and Mick Jones brought their pay cheques over to cash at Compendium. The band paid tribute to owner Nicholas Rochford in their song, 'The Prisoner', in which 'The prisoner lives in Camden Town selling revolution / the prisoner loads his tracking arm up with self-disillusion'. Compendium was more than just a bookshop. It was a place where people who shared ideas could meet, where a customer could drop by, hang out, smoke a joint with the manager, and spot Nick Cave buying poetry in the corner.

By the end of the 1990s, Camden Town was changing. Traditional bookselling was in decline, the shop was inconveniently small and narrow, and its owners planning to retire. When they sold the lease in 2000 and Compendium closed, it seemed to confirm the end of a cultural era that had begun with Centre 42. Books, however, remain in Camden, although chased into obscure corners. Black Gull Books, surrounded by tourists in the West Yard of the Lock Market, is a perfect second-hand bookshop. Walden Books, not far from the Roundhouse on Harmood Street, is inspiringly chaotic and is reputed, perhaps unfairly, to be the model for Black Books in the sitcom of the same name, lair of the nihilistically grumpy Bernard Black.

Camden Goes Punk

Although the Roundhouse brought Camden Town to wider attention, there was a host of rivals to its Camden music-scene crown. The loss of Rhythm Records, which closed in 2004, was much lamented. It was located on Camden High Street, opposite Compendium, in a space rented from the bookshop. It acted as a cultural nucleus, supplying rare and strange music to accompany the literature available from over the road. Rhythm Records was founded in the late 1970s by Jon Clare and Dave Ryner, who had already set up Honest Jon's Records in Notting Hill. They expanded into Camden, bringing their punk, reggae and rare jazz connections, and their ability to source impossible-to-find vinyl from the US, bringing in boxes of records from Chicago and the Deep South. In 1982 the founders split the business, with Dave Ryner taking on Honest Jon's Camden branch and renaming it Rhythm Records, building a credible claim to be the best record shop in London.

Skinhead boys and a punk girl at the Electric Ballroom, 1980.

At one end of the alternative spectrum, Cecil Sharp House, on the Primrose Hill side of Camden Town, is the national centre for folk music and folk dance, its logo a circle of interlocked swords. Home to the English Folk Dance and Song Society, it opened in 1931 as a memorial to folk collector extraordinaire Cecil Sharp. After hearing a gardener singing while taking tea at the house of a clergyman friend in Somerset in 1903, Sharp embarked on a career recording disappearing songs and dances, which took him on epic collecting trips to the Appalachians during the First World War. Cecil Sharp House is a village hall-style brick building, a democratic design that assumes everyone will be taking part. It was built on the site of twin Italianate villas, each with its own turret. The new building was very modern for its time, with special 'Vita' glass in the windows designed to admit health-giving ultra-violet rays. It houses the Vaughan Williams Memorial Library, the central repository of English folk culture.

At the other end of the spectrum, at least on the surface, is the Electric Ballroom behind Camden Town tube station. The Electric has gone through a series of transformations that provide a potted history of changing fashion. Built as a masonic hall, it first became a music venue in the 1930s as the Buffalo Bar, an Irish club. In the war it lost its back wall when a bomb fell on the station next door, and it was rebuilt as a much larger ballroom by Irish construction worker turned impresario Bill Fuller. He renamed it the Carousel, and booked dance band stars such as Joe Loss. It became part of an international chain of venues owned by Fuller, including the legendary Fillmore East in New York and Fillmore West in San Francisco. Despite apparently uncontroversial programming, there was a minor riot at the Carousel in 1963 when Jim Reeves refused to play on an untuned piano. The staff slipped out of the back door with the takings, leaving mounted police to deal with the angry crowd.

By the late 1970s, following hard on the heels of the Roundhouse, the Electric Ballroom had become a punk venue and rehearsal space, particularly popular with bands on the Chiswick Records label which was based at the Rock On record shop next door. The label was home to early, punk outfits featuring musicians who would soon become famous – Motörhead, Joe Strummer's the 101ers, Drug Addix (with Kirsty MacColl), Chrissie Hynde in her first band Johnny Moped, and early incarnations of Billy Bragg and Shane MacGowan. In 1978 Sid Vicious played a one-off gig at the Electric Ballroom called 'Sid Sods Off' to raise the air fares to the US for himself and Nancy Spungen – tickets which turned out to be one-way.

Camden was also closely associated with 2 Tone; the label was based on the High Street where its offices provided a hang-out for its bands. The Electric Ballroom reopened in 1979, newly sound-proofed after complaints from neighbours, with a 2 Tone evening featuring the Specials, the Selecter, Madness and Dexy's Midnight Runners. Shortly afterwards Joy Division played there twice.

Punk had also spread through Camden's smaller venues, including Dingwall's at the Lock where the diet of post-1960s pub-rock bands was shaken up by the arrival of the Clash and the Stranglers. The two bands created a punk rift when Jean-Jacques Burnel punched fellow bassist Paul Simonon and a mass brawl erupted outside the venue. The Clash, the Sex Pistols (who rehearsed in rooms under the Roundhouse) and the Ramones apparently lined up against the Stranglers and their fans. Soon the Dublin Castle on Parkway became the place to see new post-punk acts such as Elvis Costello, the Pogues and Madness (then known as the Camden Invaders).

The Camden Theatre also joined the punk and new wave scene as the Music Machine, opening in 1977. The Clash and Richard Hell played, a neo-Nazi ran on stage to punch Bob Geldof during a Boomtown Rats gig, and Bon Scott, the original singer with AC/DC, died of alcohol poisoning after a late night session at the bar. By the mid-1980s the crowds had moved on to throwing glasses at the Jesus and Mary Chain instead.

By the 1980s, the former Camden Theatre was becoming the venue of choice. A domed building outside Mornington Crescent tube station, very grand for a local theatre, it opened on Boxing Day 1900. The ceremony was conducted by local girl Ellen Terry, born in Stanhope Street (now on the Regent's Park Estate) and it initially staged plays and opera. It then became a variety theatre, the Camden Hippodrome, in 1909 and a cinema in 1913. After the Second World War, the BBC took it over as a radio theatre, recording comedy in front of a live audience. It was at the Camden Theatre that over 200 episodes of *The Goon Show* were taped between 1951 and 1960. Spike Milligan attempted to perfect the sound of a hurled batter pudding for 'The Dreaded Batter Pudding Hurler (of Bexhill-on-Sea)' episode in the Camden Theatre canteen, ordering a custard, pouring it into his sock and hurling it at the wall. A one-off final episode, 'The Last Goon Show of All', was recorded at the theatre in 1972, earning it a blue plaque.

Renamed the Camden Palace in 1982, the Camden Theatre carved out a niche as a New Romantic venue 'inspired by New York's Studio 54 but set in prosaic Camden High Street'.[15] Early electro and house music was played here, with a Friday club night hosted by New Romantic ringmaster Steve Strange. Madonna's first UK performance was at the club in 1983. Camden Palace was also frequented by early ecstasy adopters linked to Marc Almond and his band, Soft Cell. When the 1988 Summer of Love arrived, it quickly became a prime London location for acid house parties and for the 'love thug . . . former football hooligans from Millwall, Arsenal, West Ham dancing together at Camden Palace'.[16]

Neil Ansell, squatting in Camden at the time, writes about the annoyance of coming home from a long day at work to 'the squeal and throb of acid house beats in the air, and a bouncer at your door trying to charge you a fiver to get into your own home'.[17]

In the same year Dingwall's launched a night called 'Talkin' Loud and Sayin' Something', hosted by Gilles Peterson and Patrick Forge, which spawned acid jazz. Meanwhile dance crossover pioneers Soul II Soul opened a shop at No. 162 Camden High Street, across from the tube station, selling club fashion alongside 'Soul Mad Music' and '100% Dance Beats'.

A new, more multicultural version of Britain was emerging, and Camden was its home. The empty industrial and railway spaces between Camden and King's Cross were ideal venues for warehouse parties, and a sense of excitement and change infused Camden's worn-out edge lands. Once again a centre for cultural exchange and renewal, everything new in music still seemed to be coming out of Camden Town.

Britpop and the Hangover

By the start of the 1990s Camden Town had, for the first time, become self-conscious about its apparent status as London's creative capital. Cultural industry had arrived, with Muppets creator Jim Henson's Creature Shop based at No. 30 Oval Road, in former railway offices next to the Lock, and TV-AM moving into the postmodern Terry Farrell-designed studios on Hawley Crescent – a building topped with giant egg-cups, where *Good Morning Britain* was filmed. Even the Camden Road Sainsbury's was now housed in a metallic building in the fashionable high-tech style by Nicholas Grimshaw, which had replaced the ABC Aerated Bread Factory in 1985.

The brief, bizarre presence of Prince on Chalk Farm Road exemplified the growing currency of Camden as a marketing device. The New Power Generation store, at No. 20 Chalk Farm Road, offered 'a seven-day coffee shop' when it opened, something of a novelty in 1994. Crowds blocked the street and Prince waved from a balcony, but the shop, on the corner of Hawley Road, only lasted for two years. It is now inevitably a coffee chain, its path cleared by Prince himself.

However, Camden's cultural credibility was about to receive a timely shot in the arm. In 1988 the Mother Red Cap pub had been revamped as the World's End, with the Underworld music venue in the basement. Along with the Dublin Castle it became a popular location for bands struggling to get a break elsewhere. The Good Mixer on Inverness Street became the place to be seen after Blur's label, Food Records, began holding meetings there and musicians began to drink there alongside the Inverness Street market traders. Noel Gallagher moved to a flat on Albert Street from 1994, across Parkway from the Good Mixer. In her Camden-set crime novel *The Not Knowing*, Cathi Unsworth describes a thinly disguised Good Mixer, split between old and new Camdens: 'The very old, hopeless winos occupied the lounge bar and the snug, in various stages of quiet decrepitude. But the saloon bar, where there was a pool table and a tiny stage for sporadic attempts at live music, was used by the rebel set.'[18] Then the Camden Crawl festival arrived to put the new music scene on the map, running for three chaotic years from 1995 and occupying every Camden venue it could lay its hands on.

Although the Good Mixer and the Dublin Castle were the headline locations of the mid-90s, a gay pub on Bayham Street, the Laurel Tree, was the source of much of the subsequent excitement. For three years from 1993 a Saturday-night club called 'Blow Up' combined Hammond heavy lounge and 1960s beat with mod-revival haircuts and scooters, in sharp contrast to the grungier alternatives of the early 1990s. The club was patronised by members of bands including Blur, Elastica and Suede.

The Lock Tavern on Chalk Farm Road and the Stag's Head on Hawley Road (the latter now, scandalously, converted into flats) were characterful locals which attracted new clientele. The scene, labelled as Britpop in the press, quickly spiralled into parody when supposed members of Camden-based Menswear appeared on the cover of *NME* in 1993 before they had released or written any songs, or indeed formed a band. When they did, the results were underwhelming. At the other end of the spectrum were Gallon Drunk, slick-haired, undertaker-garbed, and cooler than anyone else in the room. Their music had little to do with mod worship, but they drank in the same pubs as members of Blur, musicians including Morrissey – who sang about a place 'Where taxi drivers never stop talking / Under slate grey Victorian sky' in 'Come Back to Camden' – and artists such as Peter Doig and Tracey Emin.

Like UFO before it, crowds quickly overwhelmed 'Blow Up' and it decamped to Soho, but the spotlight stayed trained on Camden.

Suggs, singer with Madness, leapt on the bandwagon with his single 'Camden Town', which offered superfluous instructions on meeting by the underground. Suggs stripped mid-1990s Camden back to its essentials – music, ethnic diversity, tourists, dodgy market goods, street drinking. By 1996 Damon Albarn was complaining that he could no longer drink in the Good Mixer because of the attention from fans. The prime Britpop movers and shakers upgraded from Camden to the Groucho Club, and were soon trading their cool for official approval from Tony Blair on the steps of Downing Street.

Daniel Lux's lowlife memoir, *Camden Parasites*, is an essential alternative account of 1990s Camden, covering material that did not fit the official story at all. Its autobiographical narrator is a self-confessed junkie who progresses from torching the Christmas tree at his local church while on Mogadon to a life of bad jobs, shoplifting, beatings, booze, drugs of absolutely every kind and, at the centre of everything, Camden. The book is full of people 'lying in bed sweating out a Turkey' in Mornington Crescent rooms unchanged from the days of Sickert, drinking codeine linctus on Albany Street, shooting up in Camden pub squats, or climbing the fence at the zoo to sleep in the goat enclosure, all the time plagued by the 'ubiquitous middle classes' determined to slum it. At one point an exposé is published in the *Sunday Mail* on the London drug scene, or as Lux comments 'part of it, being so extensive in Camden alone, it really could have filled several fat encyclopaedic volumes'.[19]

Lux died of a heroin overdose while *Camden Parasites* was at the printers. In a final posthumous touch, review copies were sent out with a note claiming that Lux, in addition to the parade of criminal activity he admits to in the book, was also responsible for vandalising the *Blue Peter* garden at BBC Television Centre.

With Britpop gone the excitement subsided, but it sparked up again in the early 2000s around Pete Doherty and the Libertines, Noel Fielding and ready-made future icon Amy Winehouse. A relieved *Evening Standard* ran a headline declaring 'Camden

Has Got Its Cool Back'. Jack White played impromptu covers one night in 2002 in the Marathon kebab shop opposite the Roundhouse, Meg White looking on. Camden Crawl returned in 2005 as a more professional undertaking, with controls on crowds and volume. This time the place everyone wanted to be was the Hawley Arms, previously a Hell's Angels pub and a market traders' hangout. The Libertines had started out from a shared flat, 'The Delaney Mansions', not far away at No. 236 Camden Road. Amy Winehouse was often to be found, either serving behind the bar or drinking in front of it, in the Hawley Arms and in most of Camden's other pubs. Photographer Robert Lang recalled that 'Pete Doherty was kind of always around'.[20] Cathi Unsworth wrote that 'Despite its down-at-heel appearance, Camden had a carnival atmosphere that set it apart',[21] and once more it all revolved around the music.

Always closely monitored for signs of cultural life, Camden Town was in the spotlight again as the press headed for the Hawley Arms, looking for an out-of-it Doherty or Winehouse for the Sunday front pages. The rapid publicity focus on Camden brought an end to any real spontaneity, and the Hawley became a parody of itself. Robert Lang said, 'I remember one night one of the Geldof sisters was there deciding who could come in. That's when we stopped going'.[22]

As though confirming the end of an era, the Hawley Arms burnt down in February 2008 in a fire that consumed the Camden Canal Market. It also destroyed the former Caernarvon Castle pub, which had fallen on hard times. To a worldwide audience at the Grammys in Los Angeles, Amy Winehouse optimistically declared 'Camden Town ain't burning down!'

While the Hawley Arms was rebuilt very quickly, the surrounding area remained in a state of dereliction for several years. In the short-term the fire added to the atmosphere, with stalls returning at Hawley Lock more ramshackle than before, graffiti paintings on the railway viaduct and parties on Castlehaven Open Space (a name, incidentally, chosen at random from a gravestone in Old

St Pancras burial ground), recalling the days when it was occupied by travellers. The handsome early nineteenth-century houses on Hawley Road were squatted, but their demolition in 2015 for large-scale redevelopment changed this corner of Camden for good.

Future Camden

Proposals to expand the tube station, demolishing both the Electric Ballroom and Buck Street Market, were fought off during the 2000s. 'Camden will never be sold' claimed Electric Ballroom owner Bill Fuller. Creeping homogenisation continues to stalk the area, cashing in on Camden's distinctiveness, and is now the greatest threat to Camden Town's continuing cultural significance.

Camden is far from immune from the inflated property prices and the development pressures that have made twenty-first-century London a difficult place to be young, creative or underpaid. The process goes back to the start of the century. The Camden Falcon pub on Royal College Street was converted to housing in 2002, and its Barfly venue relocated to Chalk Farm Road, mutating into a venue called Camden Assembly. TV-AM's egg-cup building has been demolished, replaced by more corporately acceptable offices for media giant Viacom. The Victorian building that housed Henson's Creatures Shop in the 1980s and 1990s has also been partially demolished and converted into a block of flats known as the Henson Building. The anticipated redevelopment work at the Lock Market could signal the end of an era, just as changes to the King's Road did in the 1990s or the redevelopment of Spitalfields Market in the early 2000s.

However, in spite of deadening attempts to market its history, Camden Town still attracts more teenagers than ever. The jury is out on whether they still have the freedom to make the place their own.

Notes

Chapter 1.
1. Walford 1878.
2. Camden 1607.
3. *Cary's New and Accurate Map of London and Westminster*, John Cary 1795.
4. Walford 1878.
5. Inwood 1998.
6. Palmer 1870.
7. Richard Shone in *From Beardsley to Beaverbrook: Portraits by Walter Richard Sickert*, Victoria Art Gallery, Bath 1990.
8. Booth B356.
9. Smith 1845.
10. Walford 1878.
11. Ibid.
12. Palmer 1870.
13. Ibid.
14. William Blake, *Jerusalem: The Emanation of the Giant Albion*, William Blake 1821.
15. Palmer 1870.

16. *London Courant*, 8 August 1751.
17. https://www.oldbaileyonline.org/browse.jsp?id=t17890909-95&div=t17890909-95&terms=mother%20red%20cap#highlight.
18. http://www.tate.org.uk/art/research-publications/camden-town-group/lisa-tickner-walter-sickert-the-camden-town-murder-and-tabloid-crime-r1104355.
19. https://blogs.ucl.ac.uk/library-rnid/2013/04/26/a-shirt-of-startling-hue-the-drouet-institute-and-dr-crippen.
20. Connell 2005.
21. Ibid.
22. Roger Wilkes, 'Inside Story: Last Refuge for a Killer's Mistress', *Daily Telegraph*, 30 January 2002.

23. Mavis Doriel Hay, *Murder Underground*, 1st edition 1934, British Library 2014.
24. http://www.independent. co. uk/news/uk/crime/ camden-town-rivals-world-murder-capitals-175421. html.

Chapter 2

1. Dickens 1848.
2. John le Carré, *Tinker, Tailor, Soldier, Spy*, Hodder & Stoughton 1974.
3. http://www.bphs. net/earlyhistory/ earlyinventions/index. htm#4.
4. Charlotte Mew, 'The Hay-Market', *New Statesman*, 14 February 1914.
5. Forster 1874.
6. Walford 1878.
7. Dickens 1848.
8. Rolfe 1982.
9. Thomson 1983.
10. Ramsden 1984.
11. Thomson 1983.
12. Walford 1878.
13. Davies 2013.
14. Ibid.
15. Stibbe 2013.
16. Whitehead 1999.
17. Davies 2013.

Chapter 3.

1. George Orwell, *Down and Out in Paris and London*, Victor Gollancz 1933.
2. Ibid.
3. Kavanagh 1938.
4. Thomson 1983.
5. Kavanagh 1938.
6. Madness, 'One Better Day', *Keep Moving*, 1984.
7. The Pogues, 'Transmetropolitan', *Red Roses for Me*, 1984.
8. Gallon Drunk, 'Arlington Street', *From the Heart of the Town*, 1993
9. Lux 1999.
10. Ackroyd 2000
11. Gissing 1891.
12. Thomson 1983.
13. Booth B356.
14. Ansell 2013.
15. Dickens 1839.
16. Thomson 1983.
17. Kavanagh 1938.
18. Dominic Behan, The Dubliners, 'McAlpine's Fusiliers', *Finnegan Wakes*, 1966.
19. Bill Fuller quoted in http:// www.nickelinthemachine. com/2007/12/camden-town-verlaine-and-rimbaud-a-toilet-sid-sods-off-and-the-mcalpine-fusiliers.

20. Jude Rogers, 'Don't You Be Afraid to Lie By Me: The Strange World of. . . Bert Jansch', *Quietus*, 29 February 2016.
21. Bob Davenport, 'Wild Wild Whiskey', *Down the Long Road*, 1975.
22. The Pogues, 'London Girl', *Rum, Sodomy and the Lash*, 1985.
23. Suggs, 'Camden Town', various artists, *Seeing is Believing Vol. 10*, 1995.
24. http://www.unfinishedhistories.com/history/companies/theatro-technis.
25. Thomson 1983.
26. Hill 1955.
27. Ibid.
28. Morton 1998.
29. McDonald 2000 and McDonald 2010.
30. Amelia Hill, 'Cockney Capones who ran London', *Observer*, 6 May 2000.

Chapter 4
1. http://www.zabludowiczcollection.com/uploads/files/Cathy-Unsworth-Text.pdf.
2. Robb 2000.
3. Charles de Sivry, quoted in Robb 2000.
4. Letter from Paul Verlaine, quoted in Robb 2000.
5. Robb 2000.
6. Letter from Paul Verlaine, quoted in Robb 2000.
7. Sinclair 2015.
8. Kellett 1979.
9. Dickens 1837.
10. Dickens 1850.
11. Wells 1909.
12. Ibid.
13. Mackenzie 1913.
14. For more details on the Fleet and other buried rivers, see Bolton 2010.
15. Henry Mayhew, *London Labour and the London Poor Vol. III*. Griffin, Bohn & Co. 1861.
16. Ibid.
17. Dickens 1850.
18. Booth B356.
19. Storey 1960.
20. Ibid.
21. Booth B356.
22. Walford 1878.
23. Dickens 1853.
24. For full details of Agar Town, see Bolton 2013.
25. Gissing 1891.
26. http://rsst.vpweb.co.uk/About-us.html.

27. http://www.standard.
co.uk/news/london/
squatters-sect-move-into-
camden-church-closed-
for-maintenance-9172616.
html.
28. Wells 1898.
29. Charles Marriott, 'Here
and Now', *Evening
Standard and St James's
Gazette*, 6 December 1911.
30. Walter Sickert,
'Impressionism', in *A
Collection of Paintings by
the London Impressionists*,
exhibition catalogue,
Goupil Gallery 1889.
31. Iain Sinclair, 'Metropolis
of the Disappeared',
Guardian, 2 February 2008.
32. Wyndham Lewis and
Louis F. Fergusson, *Harold
Gilman: An Appreciation*,
London 1919.
33. Richard Cork, *The Times*,
3 May 2006.
34. Hannah Rothschild, *Daily
Telegraph*, 30 September
2013.
35. Godfrey and Marcham
1952.
36. Dylan Thomas quoted in
http://www.telegraph.co.uk/
comment/9784149/Blue-
Plaque-1867-2013.html.

37. Steen Eiler Rasmussen,
London, the Unique City,
MIT Press 1982.
38. Hamnett and Williams
1980.
39. Bennett 1994.
40. Robert McCrum, 'Alan
Bennett: "I don't fret about
posterity. But some things
will last"', *Observer*, 18
December 2016.
41. Amis 1990.
42. Booth B357.
43. Sylvia Plath, 'Parliament
Hill Fields', 1961.
44. Ted Hughes, 'Last Letter',
2010.

Chapter 5
1. Miles 2010.
2. Scanlon 1997.
3. Daevid Allen, *Gong
Dreaming*, GAS Publishing
1994.
4. Boyd 2007.
5. Ibid.
6. Unidentified newspaper
cutting, 1966, http://delia-
derbyshire.net.
7. http://delia-derbyshire.net.
8. Schiele 2006.
9. http://slashseconds.org/
issues/001/001/articles/13_
sford/index.php.

10. https://50.roundhouse.org.uk/content-items/arnold-wesker-art-2.

11. *Arena: The Roundhouse – The People's Palace*, BBC Four, 23 October 2016.

12. http://spitalfieldslife.com/2016/07/17/danny-fields-manager-of-the-ramones.

13. Widgery 1989.

14. Sinclair 2013.

15. Collin 1997.

16. Ibid.

17. Ansell 2013.

18. Unsworth 2005.

19. Lux 1999.

20. Nadia Khomami, 'Robert Lang: Camden Girls of the Naughty 00s', *Guardian*, 10 July 2016.

21. Unsworth 2005.

22. Nadia Khomami, 'Robert Lang: Camden Girls of the Naughty 00s', *Guardian*, 10 July 2016.

Further Reading

Ackroyd 2000: Peter Ackroyd, *London: the Biography*, Chatto & Windus 2000

Amis 1990: Kingsley Amis, *The Folks that Live on the Hill*, Hutchinson 1990

Ansell 2013: Neil Ansell, *Deer Island*, Little Toller Books 2013

Baron 2012: Wendy Baron, *Camden Town Recalled*, Tate 2012

Bennett 1994: Alan Bennett, *Writing Home*, Faber & Faber 1994

Bolton 2013: Tom Bolton, *Vanished City*, Strange Attractor 2013

Bolton 2010: Tom Bolton, *London's Lost Rivers: A Walker's Guide*, Strange Attractor 2010

Booth B356: Charles Booth, B356 (notebook for Police District 18 [Somers Town and Camden Town] and District 19 [Kentish Town]), 1898–99

Booth B357: Charles Booth, B357 (notebook for Police District 18 [Somers Town and Camden Town], District 20 [Hampstead], District 21 [Marylebone – Christchurch to St John]), 1898

Boyd 2007: Joe Boyd, *White Bicycles: Making Music in the 1960s*, Serpent's Tail 2007

Camden 1607: William Camden, *Britannia*, Olms 1607

Camden Trust: Camden Railway Heritage Trust website, http://www.crht1837.org

Collin 1997: Matthew Collin, *Altered State: The Story of Ecstasy Culture and Acid House*, Serpent's Tail 1997

Connell 2005: Nicholas Connell, *Walter Dew: The Man Who Caught Crippen*, The History Press 2005

Connett 1992: Maureen Connett, *Walter Sickert and the Camden Town Group*, David & Charles 1992

Conyers Morrell 1935: Rev. R. Conyers Morrell, *The Story of Agar Town*, Premo Press 1935

Davies 2013: Caitlin Davies, *Camden Lock and the Market*, Frances Lincoln 2013

Denford 2003: Steven Denford and F. Peter Woodford, *Streets of Camden Town*, Camden History Society 2003

Dickens 1837: Charles Dickens, *The Pickwick Papers*, Chapman & Hall 1837

Dickens 1839: Charles Dickens, *Oliver Twist*, Richard Bentley 1839

Dickens 1848: Charles Dickens, *Dombey and Son*, Bradbury & Evans 1848

Dickens 1850: Charles Dickens, *David Copperfield*, Bradbury & Evans 1850

Dickens 1853: Charles Dickens, *Bleak House*, Bradbury & Evans 1853

Forster 1874: John Forster, *The Life of Dickens*, Chapman & Hall 1874

Gissing 1891: George Gissing, *New Grub Street*, Smith, Elder & Co 1891

Godfrey and Marcham 1952: W. H. Godfrey and W. Marcham (eds), *Survey of London, Volume 24. The Parish of St Pancras Part 4: King's Cross Neighbourhood*, London County Council 1952

Hamnett and Williams 1980: Chris Hamnett and Peter Williams, 'Social Change in London: A Study of Gentrification', *London Journal*, vol. 6, 1980, pp. 51–66

Hill 1955: Billy Hill, *Boss of Britain's Underworld*, 1st edn 1955, Billy Hill Family Ltd 2008

Holt 2012: http://www.tate.org. uk/art/research-publications/ camden-town-group/ ysanne-holt-the-camden- town-group-then-and- now-r1105679

Inwood 1998: Stephen Inwood, *A History of*

London, Macmillan 1998.

Kavanagh 1938: Patrick Kavanagh, *The Green Fool*. 1st edn. 1938, Penguin 2001

Kellett 1979: John Kellett, *Railways and Victorian Cities*, Routledge & Kegan Paul 1979.

Lux 1999: Daniel Lux, *Camden Parasites*, Unpopular Books 1999

Mackenzie 1913: Compton Mackenzie, *Sinister Street*, Martin Secker 1913

McDonald 2000: Brian McDonald, *Elephant Boys*, Mainstream Publishing 2000

McDonald 2010: Brian McDonald, *Gangs of London*, Milo Books 2010

Miles 2010: Barry Miles, *London Calling: A Countercultural History of London since 1945*, Atlantic 2010

Morton 1998: James Morton, *Gangland International*, Little, Brown & Co 1998.

Palmer 1870: Samuel Palmer, *St Pancras: Being Antiquarian, Topographical, and Biographical Memoranda*, Samuel Palmer and Field & Tuer 1870

Ramsden 1984: Caroline Ramsden, *A View from Primrose Hill: The Memoirs of Caroline Ramsden*, Hutchinson Benham 1984

Richardson 2007: John Richardson, *The Camden Town Book*, Historical Publications 2007

Robb 2000: Graham Robb, *Rimbaud*. W. W. Norton & Co. 2000

Robinson 2000: Bruce Robinson, ed. Alistair Owen, *Smoking in Bed: Conversations with Bruce Robinson*, Bloomsbury 2000

Rolfe 1982: Christopher Rolfe, 'From Camden Town to Primrose Hill', *Camden History Review*, vol. 10, 1982, p. 4, quoted in Peter J. Beck, *The War of the Worlds: From H. G. Wells to Orson Welles, Jeff Wayne, Steven Spielberg and Beyond*, Bloomsbury Academic 2016.

Roundhouse 50: Roundhouse 50th Anniversary website. https://50.roundhouse.org.uk

Scanlon 1997: Ann Scanlon, *Those Tourists Are Money:*

Rock and Roll Guide to Camden, Tristia 1997.

Schiele 2006: Jeanne Schiele, *Off-Centre Stages: Fringe Theatre at the Open Space and the Round House 1968–1983*, Nicholas Wood 2006

Sinclair 2013: Iain Sinclair, *American Smoke: Journeys to the End of the Light*, Faber & Faber 2013

Sinclair 2015: Iain Sinclair, *London Overground: A Day's Walk around the Ginger Line*, Hamish Hamilton 2015

Smith 1845: John Thomas Smith, *A Book for a Rainy Day*, Richard Bentley 1845.

Stibbe 2013: Nina Stibbe, *Love, Nina: Despatches from Family Life*, Viking 2013

Subterranea Britannica: Subterranea Britannica website. http://www.subbrit.org.uk/sb-sites/sites/c/camden_catacombs/index.shtml

Storey 1960: David Storey, *Flight into Camden*, 1st edn 1960, Penguin 1976

Tambling 2009: Jeremy Tambling, *Going Astray: Dickens and London*, Pearson Longman 2009

Thomson 1983: David Thomson, *In Camden Town*, Hutchinson 1983

Unsworth 2005: Cathi Unsworth, *The Not Knowing*, Serpent's Tail 2005

Walford 1878: Edward Walford, *Camden Town and Kentish Town, in Old and New London: Volume 5*, Cassell, Petter & Galpin 1878

Wells 1898: H. G. Wells, *The War of the Worlds*, 1898.

Wells 1909: H. G. Wells, *Tono-Bungay*, 1st edn 1909, Macmillan 1919

Whitehead 1999: Jack Whitehead, *The Growth of Camden Town: AD 1800–2000*, J. Whitehead 1999

Widgery 1989: David Widgery, *Preserving Disorder*, Pluto Press 1989

Yeates 2007: John Yeates, *N.W.1: The Camden Town Artists, A Social History*, Heale Gallery 2007

Picture Credits

2, 25, 139 Private Collection; 6 Bikeworldtravel/Shutterstock; 8 photocritical/Shutterstock; 35 Yale Center for British Art; 48 Jerome A./Panoramio; 58 Nick Catford; 62 Diageo Archive; 75 Jimmy James/Associated Newspapers; 82 National Railway Museum/SSPL; 86 Mary Evans Picture Library; 94 Museum of London/Heritage Images/Getty Images; 97, 98 Brian Shuel/Redferns/Getty Images; 109 Courtesy Brian McDonald – Gangs of London; 113 ullstein bild/Getty Images; 116 The Rimbaud and Verlaine Foundation; 130 Ron Ellis/Shutterstock; 156 Wesley/Keystone/Getty Images; 159 The National Theatre; 160 Erica Echenberg/Redferns/Getty Images; 164 Serena Wadham/Keystone/Getty Images; 167 Homer Sykes/Alamy.

Acknowledgements

I am indebted to the team at British Library Publications for bringing this book into being. Thank you in particular to Rob Davies and Jon Crabb for commissioning Camden Town; to Miranda Harrison for editing and production; to Sally Nicholls for the picture research; and Maria Vassilopoulos for promotion.

Thanks also to Paul Guest for kindly giving me access to his research, and to Charlene Coleman for her crucial Camden insight.

Index

References in *italic* indicate pages on which illustrations appear